NORTHERN ROVER

THE LIFE STORY

OF

OLAF HANSON

NORTHERN ROVER

THE LIFE STORY

OF

OLAF HANSON

by A.L. KARRAS

with OLAF HANSON

AU PRESS

Published by AU Press, Athabasca University
1200, 10011 – 109 Street
Edmonton, AB T5J 3S8

Library and Archives Canada Cataloguing in Publication

Karras, A. L.
Northern rover : the life story of Olaf Hanson / A.L. Karras.

Includes index.
Also available in electronic format.
ISBN 978-1-897425-01-5

1. Hanson, Olaf. 2. Fisheries–Saskatchewan–Love Region–History.
3. Frontier and pioneer life–Saskatchewan–Love Region. 4. Hanson Lake
Road (Sask.)–History. 5. Outdoor life–Saskatchewan–Love Region–
History. 6. Love Region (Sask.)–History. 7. Fishers–Saskatchewan–
Biography. 8. Trappers–Saskatchewan–Biography. 9. Love Region
(Sask.)–Biography. I. Title.

SD129.H35K37 2008   971.24'202092   C2008-902619-5

Cover and book design by Virginia Penny, Interpret Design Inc.

Maps prepared by Dwight Allott

Cover photograph of trees by Wayne Shiels, Lone Pine Photo

Photographs in the book are courtesy of Marylin Hanson Deschamps, except for
Saskatchewan Archives Board, p. 10: R-A4484 and p. 188: R-B7321-1.

Frontispiece: It was October of 1919 when Hanson first went into northern
Saskatchewan to hunt and trap for
a living.

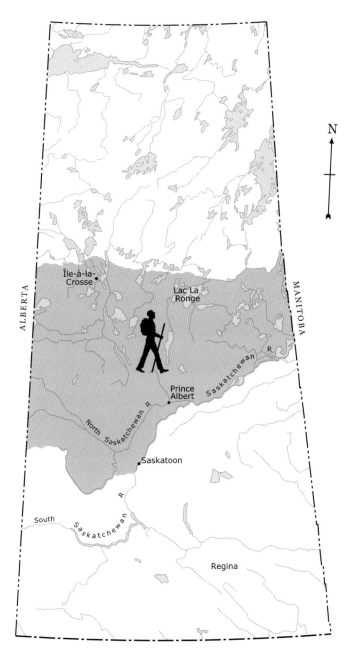

As a Rover for Department of Natural Resources in the early 1920s, Olaf Hanson patrolled this territory to enforce the provincial game laws.

INTRODUCTION

PERHAPS MORE THAN ANY other in Canada, Saskatchewan's provincial flag depicts the geographic realities of the province—a brilliant lower yellow band represents the southern prairies while the upper green background symbolizes Saskatchewan's boreal forest. A prairie lily seemingly connects the two regions. Likewise, the political geometry of Saskatchewan's mapped borders suggests an equally simple description— a near-rectangle situated squarely in the centre of western Canada, a place, at least according to the map, defined as much by longitude and latitude as by the reality of the sharply changing seasons. To most who have traveled the province, and even to most who live there today, the enduring image of Saskatchewan is that of vast grain fields slowly rusting to gold under cloudless summer skies. After all, the twentieth century was to be "Canada's Century," and that hope was firmly rooted in the southern grasslands and variably rich soil that made up the Canadian prairies. Once broken, the crops that would spring from the prairies would, it was believed, bring wealth those who toiled under those brilliant summer skies For a while at least, the hope of those who settled the prairies was shared by the nation as a whole.

But there was another Saskatchewan. And there was, and remains another brand of speculator, another type of homesteader in Saskatchewan, and indeed in Canadian history. Not all who came to Saskatchewan in the early twentieth century came for the agricultural promise of the prairies. And of those who did come to farm, take up land, make a go of homesteading on the prairie, not all stayed to live out that dream.

The powerful forces of economics and environment drove many from the land in the 1920s and 1930s. And as some were driven out by hardship and crisis, others were lured away by a more northern promise of adventure, wealth, and independence.

Life on the prairies seemed limited by seasons and surveyed homesteads. The economic potential of the prairies was similarly fettered by inequitable freight rates and fluctuating commodity prices. At the same time, the mystery of the Canadian Shield, the myriad of unnamed rivers, rocky portages, and the seemingly unending muskeg were simply too great an attraction. The north seemed boundless, a wild space then undefined by grid roads and survey stakes. In the early twentieth century, indeed until well after the Second World War, Prince Albert marked the jumping off point for so many southerners, those newcomers drawn to the north by the promise of a boreal adventure. This, and the possibility of wealth that could be gained from the land and its resources—fish, furs, and possibly minerals—proved to be a powerful motivator for many. The lure of the north, the unknown, helped many overcome the agrarian inertia of settled life on a prairie homestead.

Olaf Hanson one of these northern newcomers. For him, the trip north to Prince Albert in the years after the First World War changed his world. Unwittingly and without any great scheme or plan, he became part of or larger pattern of newcomer experience that came to shape regions, to create a new and dynamic sense of place in northern Saskatchewan. He did not venture north with a clear intent to direct the change around him, but rather he came north for far more selfish reasons. His story, the narrative that follows, demonstrates how an ever-evolving and developing sense of place in the north worked to shape his perception of northern Saskatchewan. That perception is of lasting importance for us today as we struggle to learn more about the modern north, and how that region came to shape a province, and ultimately a nation.

This is not the story of a man's triumph over nature. Olaf Hanson did not conquer the seasons or tame the northern environment, but rather he came to understand and adapt in a place he came to call home. In doing so, Olaf Hanson became immortalized not by this narrative, but by the road which bears his name—the Hanson Lake Road—the Number 106 Highway that today connects southern Saskatchewan to Creighton and Flin Flon Manitoba, and then on through other numbered highways to the provincial norths of both Saskatchewan and Manitoba. On its southern end, the Hanson Lake Road connects with the Number 55

Highway, the northern-most east–west paved highway in Saskatchewan even today. These important routes serve as a demarcation line between Saskatchewan's north and south, between two separate environments, between two worlds really.

In the years that followed the Second World War, Saskatchewan's Co-operative Commonwealth Federation (CCF) government tried to define the modern region in terms of compulsory fish and fur marketing programs. When Hanson first arrived, however, the region was a much more independent place. Before the war, individual experience was shaped not by provincial programs or southern control of the north's vast places and resources, but rather by the more immediate contrast of seasons, the cycles of not only climate, but of the flora and fauna that defined the region. These elements drew him and so many other others to the north.

Olaf Hanson was by no means unique. Hundreds, if not thousands, of others like him were drawn to the region by the same promise of adventure, the hope of wealth, and the seemingly limitless forest and its accompanying maze of rivers. After the First World War it was not uncommon for Saskatchewan's Department of Natural Resources, and especially the Game Branch, to receive inquiries from adventure-seekers as far away as England and Scotland. Most wanted maps of the region, a description of the resources contained therein, and an explanation of the limits the provincial or federal government put on one's activities in the region. Was the trapping really as good as some made it out to be? Could one find land and forest products enough to make a cabin and establish a new life in northern Saskatchewan? How far north would potatoes grow? These were the questions upon which a northern life hinged, after all, and many wanted in on it.

Many of those who did visit, travel, or work in the region also recorded their experience. Sydney Augustus Keighley's *Trader-Tripper-Trapper: The Life of a Bay Man*, P.G. Downes' *Sleeping Island: A Journey to the Edge of the Barrens*, Sigurd Olson's *The Lonely Land*, and A.L. Karras's own *North to Cree Lake* are but a few of the other narratives which explain the early twentieth century north in terms of the adventure, opportunity, crisis, and hardship which defined place in northern Saskatchewan. Hanson's story must be contextualized in time and place. When combined with these other sub-regional narratives, a clearer picture of that opaque green section of Saskatchewan's flag begins to emerge.

Hanson never intended this story to be anything more than a narrative, a winter-count, more or less, of his years roving the northern lakes, rivers, and forested muskeg of Saskatchewan. But his story leaves us with so much more than that. *Northern Rover* is as much a coming-of-age story for the author as it is for the province about which he writes. It chronicles a time in which the wealth of the provincial north became apparent, a time at which it was realized that Saskatchewan could be and was more than wheat fields and homesteads on a supposedly bountiful prairie. The fur, fish, timber, and minerals of the north, and the freedoms and challenges included therein, became apparent, not just to Hanson and other northern newcomers, but to the province as a whole. The CCF's marketing schemes, which were intended to bring economic and environmental stability to the once boom-and-bust cycles of the trade in northern staples, came with the inherent cost or coercion, or so northerners thought, of regulation and mandates. Thus Hanson's story becomes a metaphor for the costs and benefits of development in northern Saskatchewan. Just as so many were lured to the prairie west by the promise of wheat-grown wealth, Hanson and others were drawn to the north by similar, if more northern hopes. And there he, as did the province simultaneously, came of age in Canada's century.

Though Hanson's story is rich and diverse in terms of his own experience, it does not tell us as much about those who were there first. The Cree of northeastern Saskatchewan figured a larger part in Hanson's experience than we can begin to understand from his narrative. Though the interactions he does describe were at least cordial if not mutually supportive and beneficial, we cannot understand the ways in which Hanson's wilderness was pre-shaped by the native people who lived on and used the lands and waters of this story for so many generations before he and his cohort of rovers arrived in the north. None of this criticism intended to diminish the significance of his experience or his narrative, but rather it is hoped that a greater understanding of the sometimes parallel and often combined experience of adventurous newcomers and the region's contemporary native occupants will help readers understand the social and economic interaction that ushered northern Saskatchewan into the twentieth century. Here a few readable scholarly monographs will help fill in the details. F. Laurie Barron's *Walking in Indian Moccasins: The Native Policies of Tommy Douglas and the CCF* and David Quiring's *CCF Colonialism in Northern Saskatchewan: Battling Parish Priests, Bootleggers, and Fur Sharks* provide part of the context in which Hanson's story emerges—a context to which Hanson was likely too close as he lived the story which follows.

Perhaps the most striking aspect of this story is the way in which Olaf Hanson weaves his own life's story into a narrative of the northern environment. We can begin to understand the sharpness of northern seasons made real by the urgency of the first October snows, which as often as not came in late September. We should be able to understand more clearly the larger and more immediate meaning of the emergence of a snow-skies on a western horizon; we can better understand that a crisp November morning on a steaming lake does not always warm into a splendid autumn day. There is more here than a description of the difficulty of drying out an outfit after overturning a canoe on a northern lake. Hanson provides us with the graphic reality that, as so eloquently argued by Aldo Leopold in his *Sand County Almanac,* food does not come from the grocery store just as heat does not come from the furnace. Each of these commodities, just as all those in Hanson's experience, has a much more visceral origin.

Northern Rover surveys some forty years of life, experience, and change in northern Saskatchewan. Olaf Hanson's colourful, encouraging, and at times tragic story teaches us valuable lessons yet today, nearly thirty years after A.L. Karras assembled this work from Hanson's own weathered notes and vibrant memory. *Northern Rover* is no doubt enriched by Karras' own intimate knowledge of similar experience and the realities of the region itself. It is not difficult to imagine afternoons which blurred into late evenings as the two sat and reminisced about a time, as any winter evening would demonstrate, distant in years though made closer by the realities of the same cycle of northern seasons. The seasons of a human life are presented against the backdrop of a pivotal time, and a wild space made common by personal appropriation. While the road to Creighton and Flin Flon may bear his name, Olaf Hanson has given us more than a place name to remember in *Northern Rover,* he and Karras have given us the detail necessary to help us understand more about that green portion of Saskatchewan's provincial flag, and the province it represents.

Anthony Gulig
University of Wisconsin-Whitewater
October 30, 2007

PREFACE

I FIRST MET OLAF HANSON when he called at my home in Nipawin, Saskatchewan. He began by introducing himself, then said he had read my books *North to Cree Lake* and *Face the North Wind* and wished to meet their author. During the visit, he told me he had asked his truck driver to stop here on their way from Prince Albert, Saskatchewan to Flin Flon, Manitoba, where Hanson had contracted to do some blasting on the claim of a hard-rock country prospector.

Hanson at that time was well past eighty. When I asked him why he chose to continue working with explosives at such an advanced age, he answered simply, "They tell me reliable people for this work are hard to come by these days."

I was aware that during our visit Hanson had been scrutinizing me thoroughly.

I heard nothing from him until one evening more than two years later. My telephone rang, and Olaf Hanson was on the line. He wanted to know if I would write his life story. He had put together a collection of notes and it was all ready for re-writing.

After I had several meetings with Hanson and read his notes, I was convinced that he did indeed have a story to tell. In fact, he is unique among the few whites who were the real roving pioneers in the northern

Olaf Hanson and his second
wife, Margaret.

wilderness before the coming of civilization and modern technology.

In Hanson's notes there are few complaints about the intense cold of mid-winter or the flies, mosquitoes, stifling heat and humidity while packing freight on the portages in summer. In person, his face is remarkably smooth and unmarked, and there is no apparent damage to his short but still stocky frame.

An iron-legged and eagle-eyed individual, he could find his way through the unmapped wilderness alone and afoot, without a compass, in all kinds of weather, in any season by day and, occasionally, at night—if necessary.

While Hanson spent many a long period in the wilderness, he has a great interest in people, and anytime he returned and found himself among people he became the instigator and the centre of activity. He possesses unusual drive even today. His willingness to help others has been so well documented in his notes that the reader begins to take this virtue for granted.

Although he has made a host of friends throughout the north country of Manitoba and Saskatchewan during his travels, he still possesses the ability to make new friends.

A. L. Karras
Nipawin, Saskatchewan
July 10, 1981

Olaf Hanson and his second wife, Margaret, lived in retirement in an area overlooking the North Saskatchewan River in Prince Albert, Saskatchewan, until Mr. Hanson's death in 1981.

1

ROAD TO LEARNING

IT WAS OCTOBER of the year 1919 when I first went into northern Saskatchewan. While working in the harvest fields of the southern part of the province, I had made it known that I wanted to get as far away from civilization as possible to hunt and trap for a living. I had spent a few years on my homestead near Maple Creek and I had been in British Columbia, yet I had never found anything to my liking in the way of establishing a permanent occupation.

The news of my intentions spread among the harvest hands. Co-workers Ernest Stender of Kisbey, Saskatchewan and Harry Hughes, late of the state of Oregon, were as anxious to see the North as I was. We entered into a partnership.

We bought an outfit of traps, guns, skis, tent, folding camp stove with collapsible stovepipes, and all the other tools and supplies we would need to spend a winter in the bush, then shipped it all by rail to Prince Albert. Then we purchased one-way railroad tickets to this jumping-off place for the land of our dreams, a land of opportunity, adventure, and peace.

When our little group arrived in Prince Albert, we walked into a building called Lacroix Hardware on River Street. I was elected to enquire where we might find a Game Commissioner and was directed to see Mr. Andy Holmes, at that time Chief Game Commissioner for the Province of Saskatchewan. We found him at his residence, and thus began my long friendship with one of the finest gentlemen I have ever met.

That day was October 3, less than one month before the trapping

Hanson and his partners shipped what
they needed for a winter in the bush by
rail to Prince Albert, where they bought
the first three trapping licenses issued
in Saskatchewan.

season was to open officially. Holmes suggested that we locate ourselves at Candle Lake without delay and work our way north from there. We had been told that trappers must purchase trapping licenses. Holmes said that, starting with the current trapping season, trappers were indeed required to buy a license, which cost twenty-five cents each. He pointed out one advantage to the holder: if he failed to show up in the spring, then the authorities would have some idea where to look for him. That day we bought the first trapping licenses to be issued in Saskatchewan. Harry was issued No. 1; I had No. 2; and Ernest had No. 3, as that was the order in which we sat on the bench when we faced Holmes. I have no idea how many licenses were issued that year, but it gives me a good feeling to know that we were first in line. By the next year a trapper could be taken to court if he failed to be licensed, and the cost of the document had risen to two dollars.

Now it was urgent that we find someone to freight our supplies to Candle Lake. Back again at the helpful hardware store, we were told to look up a Mr. Van Ryswick, who was the proprietor of a confectionery on Eighty Street and First Avenue East. We were in luck, as Van Ryswick was expecting a friend from Henribourg who did commercial hauling with horses and would freight our supplies over the bush trail to Candle Lake. On October 5, this man, whose name I have forgotten, arrived with a wagon and a team of horses, and on the following day we left with him for his farm.

The next day the weather was sunny and mild—a grand autumn day. Our host spent that day preparing for our trip and invited us to go hunting to pass the time. It was also my birthday, and we would go hunting in order to celebrate it. We spent the morning in a fruitless search, but by mid-afternoon I had bagged my first deer in the North, a nice buck with a fine set of antlers and a grand birthday gift for a greenhorn big game hunter. The farmer got half of the meat, while we would take the remainder with us on our trip to Candle Lake.

As we slept that night, our beautiful weather left us. The next morning visibility was down to less than one hundred yards; it was snowing heavily and deep snow covered the ground, creating a great silence all around. We were unable to set out on our journey until October 10, the day it stopped snowing.

The wagon did not track well in the deep snow, so after the first day of travel we had only reached the village of Meath Park. All the way, we had walked alongside the wagon while the farmer drove his team. The flat steel wagon wheels collected snow and mixed it with the debris of autumn—grass and dead leaves. It built up more and more as the wheels turned, so we had to keep knocking off the accumulation with our axes. This made it much easier for the labouring horses.

It had not been easy on us, however. We stumbled onto the one log grocery store in the dark because the village was hidden by dense poplar and spruce timber. Only a beam of light streaming from a small window told us the store was there, but we were made welcome and, after a big meal, rolled thankfully into our blankets following our heavy day on the trail.

Half a mile on our way next morning the cleaning of the wheels had to be resumed. We came to an area where the snow had settled and by that time were more than ready for our meal of fried venison, bread, jam and coffee. (When we work hard manually for long periods, an ordinary meal becomes a great banquet.) We gave the horses a good feed of hay and oats, then men and beasts enjoyed a much-needed rest.

Continuing on our way, we crossed a creek where the crossing had a base of broken corduroy. Here snow, water, and mud gave us a bad time, and but for the abilities of the farmer, who was a good horseman, we might have become hopelessly mired. It seemed as if we had travelled twenty-five miles that day, but in reality it was only half that distance.

This was our first night of camping out. The tent was set up, but we did our cooking at the campfire because the weather was so mild a stove in the tent was not required. Once again that night our slumber was deep and dreamless.

It was the day we had planned to reach Candle Lake, but we were far from our destination when we broke camp that morning. Later in the day our party had reached the south end of Torch Lake, sometimes called Little Candle Lake. Here the wagon and the horses got stuck in a muddy creek. We tried desperately to get the wagon through, but in the end we had to unload every bit of freight.

From the creek bank, we could see that the lake had frozen over. Sure enough, when we tested the ice, we found it was strong enough to permit a man to walk safely just out from the shore.

Since our teamster was running short of hay and oats for his horses, we decided to send him home. We could now easily transport our outfit on the ice by hand sleigh to Candle Lake. The teamster reasoned correctly that he would have no problems on his return trip since he would be traveling empty and light. He left us shortly, a good man who had been eager to help us.

It was early in the day, but we made a decision to set up camp, and put up the tent, cut a supply of wood and gathered spruce bows for our beds. Now, we thought, we were in the wild North, about seventy miles from Prince Albert. We had marked the transition zone between civilization and the wilderness by observing tracks of much big game in the snow on our way to this location, and we were now in real silence for nearly all sounds were those we made ourselves.

In the morning, Ernest and I went scouting along the shore of Torch Lake. Fortunately we had brought two pairs of skates with us, and as the lake appeared to be completely frozen over, we donned the skates and in short order reached the north end of the lake, crossed a portage of about one hundred yards long and stood looking over the wide expanse of Candle Lake for the first time. Much to our surprise and dismay, for as far as we could see down the lake there was open water with white-capped waves rolling in a fair wind and bright sunshine. Until this moment we had not known the larger and deeper lakes freeze up later than do those that are small and shallow.

It was necessary to revise our plans. While in Prince Albert we had obtained maps of the area, but they lacked detail. In fact, these showed only the larger lakes: Torch, Candle, West Candle, Gull (now White Gull Lake), and White Swan. We selected Gull Lake as the site of our winter base camp, built a sleigh, and hauled our supplies across Torch Lake and then across the portage to the shore of Candle Lake. Our plan was to wait there until the lake froze over and then move to Gull Lake.

It was October 17. While in Prince Albert I had also heard that muskrat skins were selling for up to two dollars each for prime furs. Ernest and I had counted more than one hundred muskrat houses and push-ups while travelling on Torch Lake. As no other humans seemed to be about, we decided to begin our own hunting and trapping season. Harry considered that muskrats were not worth trapping; he was interested in trapping foxes, lynx and mink. During the past several days, we had seen only one coyote track, so it seemed to me there would be no fortunes made from what is termed "long-haired fur" in this country and we had better take all the muskrats we could.

The next day we made twelve muskrat sets. Before dark we had taken seven pelts and the next day ten more; by October 20 more than sixty skins. Right from the start we took care not to open too many muskrat houses to show the evidence of our trapping activity. Our group was definitely contravening the law that said the open season was not to begin until November 1.

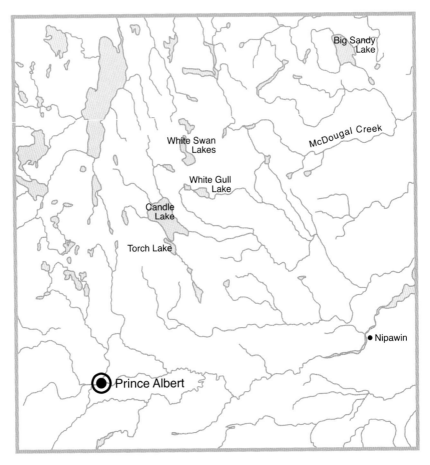

The three trappers walked alongside
the team of horses hauling their supplies
from P.A. as far as the south end of
Torch Lake and used their axes to
knock the snow and leaves from the
wagon's wheels.

Another day Harry and I explored the east shore of Candle Lake, planning to walk overland all the way to Gull Lake. We were packing a good supply of food, including bannock, coffee, sugar, and bacon. Before leaving I had hidden all the muskrat pelts by packing them in a canvas bag and securing them with stovepipe wire high in a large spruce tree. Then I buried all the carcasses deep in a muskeg.

Ernest planned to keep half a dozen traps going, just for something to do in our absence.

Our journey begun, Harry and I were slogging along shore for some distance when suddenly we came upon a Forestry Department cabin. A man named Frank Clark, the Forest Ranger, was in camp. This of course was a great surprise to us, as we had no previous knowledge of this establishment and the fact that we were camped so close to it, to say nothing of the fact that a part of Clark's duties was to apprehend violators of the game and trapping laws!

Clark showed us true northern hospitality by preparing us a nice lunch. He gave us very helpful information by directing us where to camp for the night, at an abandoned trapper's cabin situated in a large spruce bluff where the Torch River leaves Candle Lake.

As we had dallied too long under Clark's hospitality, our journey was now a bit behind schedule. It was almost dark when we reached the river, and it looked to be quite a distance to the other side. Clark had told us that we would have to wade across; there was no sign of ice there at this time of the year. Our footwear was shoe-pacs, eighteen-inch waterproof moccasins, which we removed along with our socks, then rolled up our pantlegs and started to wade, testing the water depth as we went, with the aid of two six-foot poles.

The end of October is not wading weather in the North. We hoped that the water would be not more than hip deep, yet we found it to be not more than a few inches deep all the way across! We need not have removed our footwear to walk across dry-footed. Clark had not mentioned the water's depth and the joke was on us. However, a good foot wash in the icy water could have been considered a benefit.

The night that followed is one I will never forget. We had brought no bedding. Looking around in the dark for the abandoned cabin, we were unable to locate the structure. In fact, Harry and I could not see each other when more than six feet apart. Giving up our search and a chance for a night of shelter and warmth from the stove Clark had said it contained, we built a lean-to of spruce and built a fire about seven feet long for light, cooking and to sleep beside. I was also able to find my way back to the river to fetch a pail of water for our coffee.

We slept with our clothes on, one on each side of the fire, turning over from time to time as the side away from the fire became cool. Harry was packing a shotgun on this trip to shoot small game for food. He also carried four shotgun shells in his hip pocket. During the night he moved too close to the fire until his pants caught on fire, smouldering slowly as he slept.

We were jolted awake by a loud explosion, like a gunshot, then another. We ran for the bush, wondering who had shot at us. It was not until we stopped to rest that we noticed Harry's shredded hip pocket, still smouldering. We retrieved two shotgun shells but his pants were wrecked. The balance of the night was spent in uneasy sleep, but Harry was ready to travel next morning, although he did not walk as briskly as he had on the previous day.

The morning light revealed that we had camped out only about seventy-five feet from the old cabin. Close by was a bush trail used by trappers travelling from Torch River to Gull Lake. How unnecessary seemed our problems of the past night!

Frank Clark had also informed us that he had made a trip to Gull Lake where he had found another deserted trapper's cabin, complete with a tin box stove. We were to turn left where the trail ended at Gull Lake and, upon reaching the only spruce covered point of land on the lake, we could find the cabin.

During our travels that day, we shot two spruce hens, and then finding a fine stand of low-bush cranberries, we filled a small sack with frozen fruit. We stopped for a very fine meal and proceeded to enjoy our feast. As the weather was beautiful, I am afraid we tarried too long again, for it was now too late to reach Gull Lake in daylight.

By the time we saw the lake it was getting dark. As the lake ice was thick enough for travel, we still thought we would have no trouble finding the cabin. This is when our difficulties began.

A short distance down the lake, we could see a spruce point in the dusk. On examination, we found that the point was only fifty feet wide and not suitable for a cabin site. From this spot, we could see another spruce point faintly in the distance. I wondered why Frank Clark had not mentioned this second point. As we neared the second point it looked more promising. Since it was wide enough to accommodate a cabin, we spent some time searching for one. By now it was very dark and clouding over, making our search more difficult. We still had not found the cabin, and I

Harry Hughes photographed Hanson
(left) and Ernest Stender resting as they
transported their outfit to Candle Lake
themselves using hand sleighs.

was becoming somewhat annoyed. The possibility struck me that Frank Clark had perpetrated a practical joke on a couple of greenhorns and was having a good laugh at our expense.

Again, in near dark, we made out a shape that could be another point of land. We trudged over to this place, but this point also was too narrow to be a cabin site. Once more we saw a distant point and, convinced that this finally must be our destination, we struck out again. Halfway there, while testing the ice for thickness, I saw a dark spot a few feet away. Walking over to check it, I found a round flat tin can. Lighting a match, I saw it was a new can of Nabob brand coffee! It seemed strange to find something like this out here. I lit another match and found two pairs of footprints made by people wearing moccasins and going in the same direction we were. Harry lit another match, and I put my foot in one of the tracks—it fit perfectly! Slowly, we realized that we had been travelling in circles.

Harry searched his pack to see if we still had our unopened can of coffee. The seam had parted in the bottom of his packsack and, besides the missing can of coffee, we had also lost a pound of lard.

We camped that night rather uncomfortably on the narrow point, for it was too narrow to set up camp properly. With the coming of daylight, we found that this was an island rather than a point. There are three islands in Gull Lake, lying somewhat in the shape of a three-bladed propeller. After breakfast, we went looking for our missing pound of lard, for in the North one does not take lightly the loss of such an item. We found it after an hour's search. It was on the first island we had encountered the night before.

In retrospect, we felt the loss of the can of coffee and subsequently finding it was a very valuable lesson. At night, in a strange wilderness location, one should not waste time looking for strange cabins.

In daylight, we easily found the cabin on the only spruce covered point on the lake. The structure had been well-built, but most of the moss originally packed into the chinks between the logs had fallen away. We spent the next two days and night repairing the cabin until we were satisfied that we now had a very good base camp for our winter trapping activities. On the fourth day we left to find Ernest at Candle Lake.

We set off in a happy mood with no clouds on our horizon.

It was dark when we reached the forestry cabin at Candle Lake. On seeing a lighted window, we stopped in to visit with Frank Clark. In response to our knock and much to our surprise, the door was opened by

Chief Game Commissioner Andy Holmes! We were invited in and talked about Gull Lake and the deserted cabin. Since it appeared that no one had used the cabin for at least two years and that there was no food or equipment stored there, Holmes said that we had the right to move in.

While we were talking, I glanced upward and saw some newly-stretched muskrat skins hanging among the log rafters. Quite innocently, I asked my host where he had obtained these. Looking me straight in the eye, he replied, "They're your partner Ernest's skins."

In the short interval of silence that followed, my brain was working overtime. I finally said I was very surprised that my partner had begun trapping before the season opened, all the while wondering about the safety of our first catch that I had hidden in the spruce tree, obviously undiscovered since there were fewer than thirty skins in this cabin.

Holmes told us Ernest had said that he had grown lonesome in our absence and set a few traps just for something to do. Holmes said he was sorry but he would have to prosecute Ernest for trapping out of season. There were two choices; he could be tried in a court in Prince Albert or he could appear before a magistrate. Since Holmes himself was also a magistrate, we could handle it much more quickly right here. He said he would be holding court next morning if Ernest elected to appear before him.

Holmes, as before, gave us much useful information along with a good meal before we set out the six miles to our camp.

The walk was pleasant and, usually looking at things on the brighter side, I suggested to Harry as follows:

"Ernest will be rather blue, so let's cheer him up by pulling his leg. How about we play dumb and pretend we don't know a damned thing about his problem?"

Ernest was happy to see us. We noticed that he was more quiet than usual as he set about to prepare our supper, and at no time did he make any reference to furs. When I finally asked him how many muskrats he had trapped, he squirmed uncomfortably and began to tell the story.

He had been out on the trapline when Holmes had stopped in on his way from Prince Albert on official business with Frank Clark. Before he had left that morning, Ernest had hidden his pelts under the spruce bough mattress of his bed in the tent. With no reason to suspect anything and not knowing who occupied the tent, Holmes gave the place a cursory inspection, but as he turned to leave he saw several whiskey jacks darting about, interested in something on the ground. He found that these birds were picking at several freshly-skinned muskrat carcasses.

He then awaited the return of the unknown trapper and confiscated another four skins, that day's catch.

Ernest was very worried, certain that he would be handed a jail term. Harry and I tried to cheer him by saying he would probably be fined. It was mutually agreed that we all be present for Magistrate Holmes's justice in the morning.

We reluctantly struck out that morning for our date with the law, arriving at about 11 A.M. We found that there was another client ahead of us for this chap had been found trapping at a place called "the fish station." This fellow was also uneasy. The proceedings went swiftly; Holmes handed Ernest a twenty-dollar fine, payable by January 1.

Everyone was happy once more, Holmes invited us to dinner after which we shook hands and left. There were no hard feelings; we realized that Holmes was our good friend and one who was only doing his duty.

My cache of furs still hung undiscovered in the tree, so I got away with it. However, we all learned our lesson that day and others learned the same way. If you chose to trap during the closed season, you were gambling. One year you might not be caught but the next year you would be. In my experience, I found that the trapper was invariably the loser, what with fines, confiscations, fur that was less than prime, worry, and uncertainty.

Then began the task of moving our outfit to Gull Lake. We built an improved sled and loaded our effects; we were learning, for this sled pulled easily. We worked our way northward across Candle Lake on new ice, then across country through the bush to Gull Lake. We were also learning that if you go a little more slowly real progress becomes more certain.

Things went well at our new location. By Christmas, our collection of muskrat skins numbered three hundred and sixty. As the daylight hours were quite short, we worked hard and did not miss our former surroundings. The wonders of the wilderness were our entertainment; its sounds, our music. We were very fortunate in that our cabin proved to be solid and comfortable.

At this time, a travelling fur buyer offered us $3.50 apiece for our muskrat skins. We considered this a fine price—over twelve hundred dollars in total.

Before we headed to Prince Albert to celebrate, we picked up our traps, so we had eleven more skins. We sold these in town for $5 each; which meant our loss on the first lot was over $500 and that we had learned another lesson.

In those days we had no marketing information and, because of our

In the spring of 1920 Hanson (left)
and Stender packed their catch of 120
muskrat skins in a canvas box it keep it
dry on the way to market.

isolation, little idea of prevailing market prices. We sold with much more care thereafter, as did many other trappers who had had similar experiences.

Altogether we put in a satisfactory winter—it was a pleasant existence and we made a fair amount of money, considering the purchasing power of the Canadian dollar at that time. Although we trapped the Candle and Gull Lake country, I made two trips on foot to White Swan Lake to the north.

That year I shot my one and only timber wolf in all my years in the North. I had occasion to hear them howl frequently, yet they stayed clear of men as a rule.

The month of May came all to quickly for us, and the trapping season was over. When we arrived in Prince Albert with one hundred and twenty muskrat skins, we were shocked to learn that most buyers would not quote a price, for the bottom had fallen out of the fur market. One buyer offered us twenty-five cents each—what a disappointment! I had talked to another trapper and learned that he had received an average of $2.10. We made a mad dash for this other buyer, and our average price there was the same as quoted by our trapper friend.

A celebration immediately followed, of course.

Somewhat later I learned what had happened in the fur market. I met our buyer a week later. Three days after he bought our furs, he received a telegram from his head office instructing him to stop buying pelts. An American firm in St. Louis had tried to corner the fur market. It was a vast organization. Fur prices reached fantastic heights and musk-rats went to $5—a rise of four hundred per cent—over the price in the previous season.

Trappers, excited by the vision of fortunes to be made, headed for swamps, skinning their catch around campfires at night and jotting down mythical values in pocket notebooks. Traders were taken in, since the delays in communication from their parent firms delayed the news of the market crash for weeks, so that they paid the high prices when actually the market did not exist.

The St. Louis firm was forced into bankruptcy, and it was said a bank failed as a result. Assets of the firm were liquidated, their vast stores of fur sold to the highest bidder until this commodity became unsaleable because of the oversupply.

My partners now left to visit their homes: Ernest to Glenavon,

Saskatchewan, and Harry to Brandon, Oregon, where he wanted me as his partner to develop a dairy farm. He needed more money, so I gave him a payment of $500 for fifteen acres of land in his home state, but I did not go to Oregon.

2

FOREST RANGER

WITH THE END OF THE First World War, Canadian veterans were returning home, and one met them here and there in the North. The Canadian Government was working hard to place these men into civilian life by way of jobs, farmland and training. One such veteran whom I had met in the previous winter was Bert Vanderkracht.

My partners had visited with Bert during our travels and had shared experiences and stories. They had included my role in some of these tales and represented me as a woodsman of some ability. Actually, though I was learning a great deal, I would hardly have considered myself an experienced woodsman at that time. Still, Bert seemed interested and wanted to meet me.

In February of that year they met again, but this time I was in their company. Bert asked me about my plans for the coming summer.

"I really don't know," I said. "I haven't given it much thought. Something always turns up."

Bert wanted to stay in the North and he came up with an interesting plan. Being a war veteran he felt he could get a government job as a forest

Hanson on fire patrol with the first dog
he purchased, photographed near the
Fire Ranger cabin at Candle Lake.

ranger. He admitted he knew little about the work involved but thought if we teamed up he would try to get me appointed as his assistant, and I could teach him to be a woodsman. I readily agreed because I would then be drawing regular pay for doing work I enjoyed. After Bert sent in the applications, we went our separate ways until one day I received word that our applications were accepted and we would be assigned to the Candle Lake District. I was delighted, and thus began my life as a forest ranger's assistant.

Included in the course I laid down for my friend was how to travel across country through the bush without getting lost. In this activity we did a great deal of walking; in the beginning, we were on the move four or five days a week. I tried to teach him what I knew and stressed that in the North it is essential to always be certain of the direction in which you are travelling. This is particularly important on cloudy days when the sun is hidden and other signs become obscured.

Wilderness knowledge can save your life in this harsh climate, and life can be comfortable here if you follow the rules. I felt that Bert was learning the basics of survival, and he proved to be a good student. I taught him what I knew of wilderness survival, but I still had many things to learn at that time and added to my woods education as the years went by.

During that summer I instructed Bert as follows.

"In sunshine you have of course the sun to direct you while travelling in the woods. In cloudy weather many outdoorsmen use a compass, and I strongly urge you to use one too. No one should be in the woods without one. There will be occasions when you find yourself without a compass: by forgetting it at home, because of accidental loss or breakage, or because of some other reason, such as when you become separated from your hunting partner, who has the only compass.

"Imagine it's a nice sunny day, so you separate and go in different directions. There is nothing to worry about for the sun is out. You are interested in finding game, and two or three hours pass by. Now you decide to return to camp, but when you look for the sun the sky is overcast. If it's wintertime, it may begin to rain or snow. You have no compass, for your partner has it. You decide you will have no difficulty in finding your way back to camp, and you strike off quickly in the direction you think your camp is located. After you have walked for an hour or two, you still haven't seen any of the landmarks noted on your way in. It is getting dark. You rush on instead of stopping for the night and making a fire. You panic and run. No one ever finds you again.

"I have met several men who told me that while lost in the bush they have walked all night hoping to get back to camp. The lucky ones are found, but some vanish forever.

"I was raised in bush country. I never carry a compass because I have learned to find my way without one. From the age of seven until I was sixteen, I lived in wilderness country in northern Minnesota. There is a lot of aspen or white poplar in this region. Several old woodsmen told me that I would never lose my way in cloudy weather if I studied the white poplars. 'The south side of the bark is white and the north side is green,' they told me.

"By the time I was sixteen years of age, I could keep my directions just by glancing at the poplars as I walked. I found this more convenient than taking out a compass and stopping to take a reading. My method meant that I did not have to stop to check on my directions.

"During the winter of 1914–1915 I had been trapping in the Cariboo district of British Columbia. There I found that spruce and jack pine were covered with moss and lichens on the north side to about one or two feet above the butt of the tree. I could now 'read' poplar, spruce, and jack pine, and I never had any problems finding my way while in that region.

"However, when I came to northern Saskatchewan that first winter, we had snowfall in excess of three feet. In jack pine and spruce forest I could dig down to find the moss and lichen growth, but I found this too time-consuming. I began to examine the trees more carefully, and I discovered more direction indicators. The south sides of spruce and jack pine trees I found have loose scaly bark; on the north side the scales are much tighter. Then I found that spruce and jack pine have lichens growing under the bark scales on the north sides of the trees. The bark is brighter and more glossy on the south sides. I was astonished that I hadn't noticed these signs before. Now I was all set to forget about carrying a compass.

"Occasionally I was still out in my directions, but never enough to become lost. Every year there was news of someone who had been lost in the bush. That was when I began to examine all kinds of trees and anything growing that might have some indicators to show north and south. I wasn't long in finding the north and south sides of all varieties of trees. Tamarack, I learned, have dull-coloured bark on the north and bright glossy scales on their south sides. Birch, one of the most difficult trees to read as a direction finder because of its white bark all around, has a few specks of lichen on the north side of old trees. Many large birch have split bark, always on the south side. These cracks are caused by alternate thawing and freezing in warm and cold weather. There are days in March when the sun shines warmly on the south side of the trees, thaws the bark on that side only, and when the thermometer plummets in the night, the bark is refrozen and splits open. Willow and alders show glossy bark on the south sides and dull bark on the north sides.

"Never look for direction signs from trees that are standing close together in thick bush. Here the tree trunks are in perpetual shade, the boles never exposed to direct sunlight. Only trees with an open exposure to the sun will show its effects on bark colouration. Trees on the edge of any old clearing, such as on a lake shore, river bank, edge of an open muskeg or rim of an old burning will give you the signs. An open muskeg is one of the best locations because the small stunted tamaracks will give you a very good reading. There are lichens growing up from four to seven feet from the butt on the north side of each tree. Tree signs of course cannot be found in burnt stands of trees.

"During daylight travel, keep track of your direction constantly and the length of time you walk in each direction, assuming that you are carrying a watch. When it is time to return, you can judge very closely the distance and direction to your destination.

"I have been told by good woodsmen that all trees have more limbs on the south side. I will agree that many trees have more limbs on the south side, but others do not, and lots of trees have more limbs on the north side! Using this method will eventually get you lost in the woods.

"Anyone who frequently travels on foot through wooded country should practice keeping his or her direction by reading the trees in sunlight as well as in cloudy conditions. You will learn that you are determining north and south as a sixth sense without realizing you are doing so. As a beginner you will be uncertain and slow in your progress and finding your direction. But each day will find you more adept and improved.

"Let me stress again that you should carry a compass because it may one day save your life. There are places, however, where a compass will keep you travelling in all directions. In Canada's Pre-Cambrian Shield, should you find yourself in an area of magnetic iron ore, the compass needle may point to any direction, but a lone tree will still give you a reliable direction reading.

"I have experienced all these things about direction finding. I never worry about becoming lost, and I never have been lost. Several times when I was looking for big game or fur animals and new trapping territory, I would find myself ten or fifteen miles from camp when darkness overtook me. If the night was clear, I set out for camp using the North Star or the Big Dipper as a guide. If travelling through thick bush, I could always get a glimpse of the Little Dipper to the east, and sooner or later I would come upon one of my trails leading to camp.

"Always remember not to panic in any situation.

"When you leave your camp in the morning to travel for a day in the woods, take enough food for at least three meals and a tin tea pail with a wire bail or handle to hang it over the camp fire. Any four- or five-pound tin will do. It will be a great comfort to you to make tea or coffee if you have to camp out.

"If the weather is cloudy, I make camp early. I always carry a good supply of matches in a waterproof matchbox, as well as a belt axe and a hunting knife. Matches are most important and could mean the difference between life and death. A mid-winter camp without them means that you will have to keep running in a small circle to keep from freezing to death.

"Any time you are overtaken by darkness in cloudy weather when you are more than one mile from your camp, trail or road, stop for the night. Try to find a place where there is some dry wood, also some green spruce. Make your fire first. By its light you can cut a supply of wood and build your shelter. To make a good lean-to, look for two trees standing on level ground and eight to ten feet apart. Cut a pole two or three feet longer than the distance between the two trees. Now cut two poles eight or nine feet long; trim off all limbs except the top one on each pole, as this limb is used to hold up the cross pole against the tree on each side of the shelter. Place poles about a foot apart against the cross pole, and seal off any wind by piling spruce boughs on the slanting poles. Always build your lean-to so that the wind is blowing towards the fire and away from the lean-to so that you and the fire are in the shelter of the wind.

"Now cut a good supply of spruce boughs for your bed and to keep your feet out of the snow. Keep your fire about seven feet in length. You will find yourself reasonably comfortable and will even get a few naps of sleep in weather that is minus forty degrees Fahrenheit. It will give you a lot of satisfaction and confidence to know that you have successfully spent the night under extreme conditions and found your way to camp next morning."

After about two months on the job, I dreamt up a challenge for Bert. I suggested that we walk from Candle Lake to Montreal Lake, a round trip of some fifty miles. His eyes lit up with interest and we prepared for this trip with enthusiasm and joy.

The whole season's fur catch, prepared
and stretched, looked pretty impressive.

Our needs on the trail were becoming simpler. Our food was bannock, tea, coffee, a tin of jam, a can of butter and a few tins of pork and beans. I knew we would feel we were eating like kings.

We paddled the canoe to the west end of Candle Lake. That night we camped on the lakeshore and talked a long time in the twilight, for a fine bond of companionship had built up between us in the past weeks.

I estimated that we should reach Montreal Lake in one day of travel. I realized this was a challenge as we started off next morning. Shortly, we came upon a blazed trap-line trail, which we followed, for it led generally northward. These trails, I knew, could be very helpful when travelling in strange territory. By 1 P.M. this track became more distinct and continued to lead to the north. The training of the past weeks became evident now, for we walked at a brisk pace, covering a great deal of territory. Twice we stopped to rest and to enjoy a sustaining lunch.

At dusk we were elated to arrive at the shore of Montreal Lake. We felt a sense of some achievement. We were as yet far from our destination, the village called Montreal Lake, but felt confident of reaching our goal in due time. By way of celebration, we enjoyed the third lunch of the day, exuberant in our success.

Our search for the village led us toward the southwest as we followed the lakeshore for three hours. It was quite dark now, and we were dead tired. When we sat down to rest, we heard the barking of a dog from some distance away, a most welcome and wonderful sound, for it meant the village must be very close now. Soon we halted, as we came to the bank of a river that looked as if it could be very deep; crossing a strange river on foot in the dark is very foolhardy. We felt there must be a bridge to the village somewhere but searched in the dark to no avail.

Near the riverbank someone had been cutting hay. As we had brought no bedding, we made beds in the warm aromatic hay coils and fell into such a deep sleep that the sun was high in the sky when we awoke to see before our eyes the village we had been seeking in the dark.

We prepared an unhurried breakfast, savouring our food deliberately. I always particularly enjoyed breakfast when camping out; the food seemed to taste better and the coffee was delicious.

It was no problem to find the bridge in daylight. We followed the road to the village, a small trading centre which served the native population and the occasional white trapper or traveller.

Our first call was to the ranger station, but the Forest Ranger was away and no one could tell us when to expect his return. Next we visited with the manager of Revillon Frères Trading Company at the trading post, a man we had met previously. Glad to see us, he invited us to stay for a few days. In those days strangers were always welcome, for with them came news of other places and other people. We rested there that day and the next night since our feet were sore from our long walk.

On the return trek to Candle Lake it was a joy to walk among the northern pines in warm sunshine. We made the trip in one long day, including the fourteen-mile canoe trip to our ranger station.

When you arrive at a goal that is difficult to attain, you always get tremendous joy from the achievement. By walking we had enjoyed the good sounds of nature, such as the glad song of birds at dawn and their soothing notes in the evening stillness. We had inhaled the good smell of decomposing leaves returning to the earth to nourish new growth.

During the entire fire season, we had only one small fire outbreak to put out, that near the community of Paddockwood, and we extinguished it in one day's work. This was in contrast to normal seasons, when prolonged hot dry weather changes the northland to a vast tinder box, when rangers and fire fighters work around the clock for long periods of time, and when situations arise where they are in real danger for their lives.

For the first time that September we heard the mating calls of the bull elk. Their bugling sounded from near and far across the hills and swampland, now in bright autumn array. I was so intrigued by the sound that I began to practice imitating it by using my voice and cupping my hands around my mouth. As elk were very plentiful that fall, I had an excellent opportunity to practice the sound. After a great deal of practice, I called one quiet evening and was immediately answered by a bull elk. After dark I listened to elk calling from several directions. When the calling ceased, I bugled and soon all the bulls were calling again.

That season I heard only two moose calls. It had not been a good season for them, and we saw little moose sign either.

This had been my first autumn in the North, and I found it to be my favourite of the seasons. The autumn colours were particularly vivid that year; poplar and birch turned bright yellow and the underbrush became a study in red, gold, russet, and beige. When these began to fade, the threadlike foliage of the tamaracks (a species of larch) splashed the swamplands with a yet more vivid yellow. It was then that I committed my life to the North.

The fire season ended on October 15, as did our jobs. The appointment had been most valuable to me, for besides the salary and the experience, it seemed like a prolonged summer of continuous outdoor vacation.

Bert and I were at loose ends for a time but finally settled into the Gull Lake cabin for the trapping season. We did rather well financially, but Bert did not enjoy trapping, for often the animals suffered greatly due to the tortures inflicted by the leg hold trap, which was the only model available at that time.

After Christmas, Bert went commercial fishing with a chap named William Schrader at Candle Lake. This occupation did not appeal to me because it was hard and punishing work in the dead of winter.

I would resume trapping. I felt much as Bert did about the cruelties of traps, yet trapping was giving me a livelihood and providing a logical reason for being in the North, the place where I wanted to be.

3

FROM POACHER
TO GAME GUARDIAN

NEAR THE END OF 1920, William Arenth arrived at Candle Lake from Oxbow, Saskatchewan. Bill was new to the North. We joined in a trapping partnership located at Gull Lake, in my headquarters of the previous trapping season.

By that time, I had bought three dogs and a toboggan, so we had no problem transporting our supplies. Bill asked me what I intended to do about dog feed.

"Don't worry, Bill," I said, "I can get a moose any time I want one." In my first winter at Gull Lake, I had hunted moose with little success and a great deal of difficulty. Then one day I had met a Native hunter on the trail. Over a cup of tea at the campfire, he explained to me exactly how to track moose in the snow. Thereafter I did better. Sometimes I failed, but I gradually improved to the point where I was successful in two out of three attempts.

The news of my hunting success began to spread. Many trappers and commercial fishermen came to me for a moose or a caribou, and I began to shoot moose for anyone who asked me to get moose meat. In fact,

Hanson spent the winter of 1920/21 trapping and hunting on the north shore of Gull Lake.

I was spending more time hunting than trapping the season I was with Bill Arenth. Caribou and moose were very plentiful; for an experienced hunter, it was like going out into a pasture and shooting a standing steer.

Thus I became adept at hunting moose, the only big game animal I ever learned to bag consistently. One little secret I kept to myself for years was that there is little point in trying to track a moose on a calm day. Go when a stiff breeze is blowing.

Bill had bought a new ten-by-twelve foot tent with a stove and all the necessary comforts for a long stay anywhere we chose to set up camp. With our dogs to haul the outfit, we now had an early version of the mobile home, and so we moved about a fair bit that winter. I had grown tired of the White Gull cabin and wanted to look at some new country. One day we loaded everything and moved eastward down White Gull Creek a distance of some twelve miles. In 1918, a big forest fire had burned through this area, and we found a nice green stand of spruce on the creek bank, close to lots of dry, fire-killed wood. We reached this spot on the last day of 1920, and here we would establish a new comfortable home.

To get the site ready we first had to get rid of the snow, and there was a lot of snow. First we tramped down an area about fifteen feet square. Then we lit a big fire on the site. By the time all the snow had melted off, it was 2 A.M. Then we had to clean up the resulting mess of ashes, so that the site was not ready until 3:30 A.M. One thing that you learn in the bush is patience.

We had not taken time for a meal. Now we celebrated the New Year by having a hearty lunch, which we dragged out to include another smaller lunch. Then we carefully set up the new tent and installed the fine airtight heater. We had worked a double shift even by our own standards.

New Year's Day we would celebrate by sleeping in very late. The beds were prepared, the stove was banked for the night, and we fell exhausted into our sleeping robes. What was left of the night would be comfortable.

I was the first to awaken that morning. I pulled my robe off my head, and as I began to move I felt something wet. When I threw off the robe, I promptly received a face full of snow! For a few seconds I just sat there trying to remember where I was while large snowflakes were falling on my upturned face, so that I could scarcely see anything.

My wits were returning. Snow covered our beds, and the tent was hardly there—the roof completely gone, the stovepipe leaning on what was left of one tent wall, and the stove lying on its side. Sparks from the stovepipe had ignited the new cotton canvas as we slept. The roof had burned off, but the ends of the tent were intact.

Bill was still asleep. Now I called out, "Wake up Bill, Happy New Year!"

I sat down as he pulled the covers off his face and sat bolt upright. Snow fell on his head; then he scrambled to his feet.

"My tent! My new tent," he shouted.

It was a poor beginning to the new year and a great disappointment, yet we were fortunate we had lost only the tent. We might have awakened that morning playing a harp duet.

Bill wanted to return to the old cabin but I had another idea. The weather was rather mild, so I suggested that the tent could be repaired, and we got to work. From the toboggan we removed the carriole (a six-by-twelve foot canvas tarpaulin) which we tied in place over the ridgepole to make a partial roof. We swept off our beds, set up the stove and, though there was daylight showing here and there, we were back in business. Back at the Gull Lake cabin, Bill had another, smaller canvas, and there were a number of empty flour sacks. I returned to the cabin with the dogs and brought back this material. That night the repair job was completed, but the result was not nearly as fine an abode as we had had before the fire. Later that winter Bill made a trip to Prince Albert, returning with a new twelve-by-sixteen sheet of canvas from which we effected permanent repairs to the tent.

That winter was not very profitable as far as trapping was concerned. By early April I got a bit bored and decided that a trip to the fish station at Candle Lake would be in order. Every winter a couple of cabins there were the habitation of commercial fishermen and trappers, so on a visit there one might find from two to six men who were willing to play cards or just have a friendly visit. It was also the headquarters for the area mail delivery and pick-up and a place to learn any news from "outside," as we called civilization. The isolation of the North makes people very hospitable indeed. With a group like that one can have a great visit with never a dull moment.

I was greatly surprised to find a message waiting for me. Chief Game Commissioner Andy Holmes was asking me to call at his home the next time I should be in Prince Albert. During my conversation that evening with the fellows at the fish station I mentioned the contents of this message.

The general opinion of these gentlemen was that I would be as crazy as a hoot owl to go calling on the chief game commissioner. In all probability he had collected a fine lot of evidence about all the big game I had been killing out of season. I too felt this was probably the reason I was being called in, yet above all things I did not want to be running away from people. I decided right then to go make my call, face the music, and pay my fine. After all, Holmes's job was to apprehend law-breakers, a role I fit exactly.

I left for Prince Albert and in due course arrived at the office of Chief Game Commissioner Holmes. I was very apprehensive about the outcome of this morning's events, for there had been a general tightening of the hunting and trapping regulations. Fines had been getting larger, and I had made little money that winter.

Mr. Holmes seemed very pleased to see me. After a few words of greeting and a bit of small talk, he went directly to the reason for his request that I call. He was offering me the position of Provincial Game Guardian!

To say that I was surprised would have been a huge understatement. I was dumbfounded! When my wits returned, I mumbled something about my inexperience at such work. Holmes assured me that I had nothing to worry about, for he personally would give me that training.

All this time my conscience had been bothering me. I was thinking about all the big game I had killed out of season, and I began to squirm. Finally I blurted out, "Mr. Holmes, I have violated the game laws many times, which makes me a poor candidate for the job."

Holmes smiled kindly at me and replied, "Mr. Hanson, we have all violated the game laws. Almost everyone in the country has done so, but we are now entering a new era where we must preserve our wildlife for the future. If you are engaged in enforcing the game laws, you will train and convince yourself that you shouldn't violate them."

"Actually," he continued, "because of your illegal activities, you are probably better qualified than most candidates to thwart poachers for you understand their methods and what to look for. Besides, your woods experience makes you a natural."

We talked for a long time then. When I left, I had accepted the job and was to begin May 1, 1921.

For the new job I was to supply my own team of horses and a wagon. I was next thing to being dead broke, but somewhere in my belongings was the deed for the land in Oregon that Harry Hughes had sold to me. I wrote to him and explained my need for ready cash. Would he buy back the fifteen acres of land? Within a short time, as long as it took for both letters to be delivered, he sent his letter and cheque. He strongly urged me to not sell the land if possible, because the West Coast Highway passed by the corner of the property. Real estate values were rising in Oregon, he wrote, and he was certain that the place would one day be worth a lot of money.

I am afraid that at the time I could not have been less interested in Oregon real estate. I was also in dire need of funds to buy my team and wagon, so I cashed the cheque and sent Hughes the land deed. Many years passed before I heard from him again. By that time he owned a profitable dairy farm at Coquille, and what were once my fifteen acres overlooking the wide Pacific Ocean had reached values to stagger the imagination.

The same day that the cheque arrived, I bought a team of horses, a wagon, and two sets of harness, all for $300. I picked up my camping outfit at Candle Lake where Bill Arenth had left it, returned to Prince Albert, and was ready to go to work by May 1.

My working area was quite large. My first assignment was to patrol with team and wagon from Prince Albert to Shellbrook, west to Mistiwasis, north to Big River, and then back to Prince Albert.

I had been instructed to prosecute the big offenders, and my first priority was to catch a man who operated a country store at Stoney Lake (Delaronde Lake) near Big River. He bought big game carcasses from hunters and resold them to the locals. Meat was hard to come by for many residents, so that venison had a ready market. Any enforcement of the game laws would be a hard and painful process. Flagrant violations had been the rule for many years, and I realized that I would be disrupting a way of life. As it turned out, I was able to gather enough evidence to take the case to court. This took place in Big River on June 9, 1921. The court room was packed with local residents, and every person charged was fined from ten to two hundred dollars, depending on the extent of his misdemeanours. The storekeeper was required to pay the highest fine.

I learned quickly that enemies came easily in my line of work. By the end of my stay in Big River, I had no friends, and really I could not expect to have any, but it did bother me. In any frontier town there is apt to be a reckless, hard-drinking, and vocal element who would think nothing of running me bodily out of town—a situation similar to the popular understanding of the relationship between hillbilly moonshiner and revenuer. Big River was exactly such a town at that time. I was lucky to get out of town peaceably and with a whole skin.

On my way back to Prince Albert, I stopped at Canwood and at all the

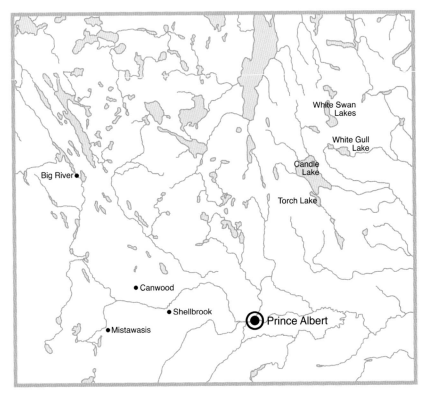

Beginning May 1, 1921, Game Guardian
Hanson patrolled from Prince Albert
west to Shellbrook and Mistawasis,
north to Big River, then back to P.A.

lesser stations along the way. The news of the court cases had preceded me, and when I finally arrived in Prince Albert, all our staff shook my hand and congratulated me on a job well done.

These plaudits brightened my outlook considerably. I felt that I had been instrumental in demonstrating that the laws are applicable to everyone and that I was contributing to game conservation now in recompense for the violations I had perpetrated before. If we had continued without regard for our rich natural heritage, there would have been nothing left for the future. These thoughts encouraged me greatly, and I decided that I was seriously interested in my work.

Later that summer I was sent down to the prairie region. The position of Game Guardian was new in the area, and I was kept quite busy. I sold my team and wagon and bought a Model T Ford car. Then I was able to patrol by car on the roads and wagon tracks, and on horseback elsewhere. Rent for a horse and saddle was one dollar a day. The work became easier, and I was successful in obtaining a fair number of convictions.

In 1922 more men were hired to our staff. I was appointed as a Rover with no particular district, with my expenses paid by the Game Branch of the Department of Natural Resources. My territory ran from Prince Albert south to Saskatoon, then west to the Alberta boundary, north to Ile-à-la-Crosse, east to Lac La Ronge and the border of Manitoba, south to the Saskatchewan River and then westward back to Prince Albert.

I roamed this immense region using every available form of transportation: train, car, horseback or horse-drawn vehicle, dog team, skis or snowshoes, canoe in the open water season, and otherwise, just plain afoot. Aircraft were so new in the north that they were not yet available to the game guardians.

I got to know many people well, whether they were northern Natives or southern homesteaders. Many of the people became lifelong friends. I was always welcome at their homes, where the hospitality was of the highest order and a pleasant diversion from the long lonely patrols. The best food was prepared because of the company. It was rather amusing when I was served venison that had been shot out of season. Fresh meat on the table before the season is legally open must have been taken illegally. When this happened, I made a point of thanking my host and hostess for the "good beef."

I am sure some people chuckled at my departure because I was so gullible. I recall one family in particular. One night I had stopped at their home and ate ground meat mixed with mashed potatoes. This was before the hunting season had opened. The next year I stopped at the same place again, but during the hunting season. I was served a fine moose steak. As we sat visiting after supper, the lady of the house asked me if I could distinguish by taste the various wild meats, such as venison, elk, moose and caribou, from the taste of beef.

I answered at once, "Not only can I do that, but I can tell by taste any kind of wild meat, and identify it as deer, moose, elk, caribou, or whatever it may be."

Right away I knew I had overstated my ability in this regard.

"All right then," said my hostess. "What kind of meat did we serve to you here last year?"

I reflected for a few seconds back to the ground meat I had eaten there a year ago and gave it a guess.

"Well, that meat was elk."

By the surprised look on their faces, I knew I was right. However, I neglected to tell them I had also known the elk had been taken before that year's hunting season had opened.

Hardship and oppressive poverty were rife in the whole northland at that time. Had it not been for the big game available in the area, many homesteaders would have found life there untenable. It is certain that their growing children benefited greatly from the supply of fresh meat. I could not fault these people for killing game illegally if it was for their own use, and there were many times my eyes failed to see what I was being paid to observe.

Many varied and interesting things happened to me during those early traveling days. Patrolling by dog team appealed to me, for dogs can be great company when one is otherwise alone. Sometimes I rode on the toboggan, but most times I walked ahead on snowshoes to break trail and to find the best route when travelling overland. There were many thick stands of young growth where I had to do some cutting to get the toboggan through. A good day's travel was from ten to twelve miles.

I purposely stayed clear of established trails. These wandered a good deal, as trapping and hunting trails meander through the countryside. The paths that I chose were as straight as possible, a course which led me into untravelled territory with interesting happenings and adventures along the way.

In wilderness travel the sighting of big game was the rule rather than the exception that it is today. I came upon vast winter feeding grounds of moose where the great beasts seemed only mildly surprised to see me

A good day's travel for Hanson and his
dog team was from ten to twelve miles
when on patrol in the winter of 1921.

pass by. Woodland caribou gave me a shy but similar reception when I crossed endless bog and muskeg country. Inquisitive deer took a step or two in my direction before they bounded off, white flags aloft. In uncut prime stands of white spruce, I travelled as in an enchanted forest from Grimm's fairy tales. Among the big boles, I was an insignificant figure threading my way through the constant gloom.

As each evening approached, I would keep an eye open for a suitable place to spend the night. I choose the spot based on the availability of dry wood for a fire and green spruce trees for my bed. It sounds rather primitive as far as living goes, but I enjoyed it all immensely. The nights were filled with the hearty perfume of balsam and wisps of smoke from the campfire. There were comforting sounds to lull me to sleep—the hooting of owls, the crackling fire, the coyotes howling from far-off hunting grounds. What a rich man I was!

I look back fondly on one particular experience. That day I was travelling on skis ahead of my dogs across country far into the wilderness. I camped overnight and continued on my way the next morning. Late in the day, I came upon a fresh ski trail that was easy to travel upon and led generally in my intended direction.

It was near dusk when I came upon a fine stand of white spruce. Tucked away to one side, I found a small log cabin. An inviting column of white smoke rose from the chimney. As there was no one about outside, I knocked on the door and, receiving no reply, I opened the door, and entered the cabin.

My nose was greeted by a strong odour coming from the direction of three large wooden casks at the far end of the cabin. On investigating, I found all the barrels to be full of fermenting mash, and a small distillery was in full production.

My job had nothing to do with the Prohibition Act, which was in force at the time—or with stills or home-brew. I chuckled to myself, unhitched the dogs, and prepared to feed them for the night.

I had just finished feeding my dogs when I saw two men enter the clearing from the opposite side from whence I had come. Two more men followed them. When they saw me, they all stopped suddenly and looked very frightened. I shouted what I thought was a friendly greeting but received no reply.

Finally I asked if I could stay for the night. Since hospitality was the rule in the North, one chap nodded his head and said yes, he thought I could. While they removed their skis, one fellow asked me if I was a trapper.

"No," I said, but offered no further information.

Then one turned to the other and wondered aloud in Swedish who I was. He also wondered what I was doing there. Norwegian is my native language, but I understand and speak Swedish as well. While I understood him perfectly, my English was almost without any tell-tale accent, for I had not used my native tongue very much since arriving in Minnesota from Norway at an early age.

I did not indicate that I had understood what had been said but just stood there and put on my friendliest smile. They watched the dogs eat for a while, then asked me to come into the cabin. After we had sat down, I was asked if I was a forest ranger.

"No," I replied again and once more volunteered nothing.

They looked very worried now and began to fidget uncomfortably. Then one said to another, "It is no use trying to hide anything now; it's too late."

I decided then that my little joke had gone far enough. In Swedish, I told them that they need not worry about me. I was a provincial game guardian and as such I had nothing to do with the Prohibition Act. I had seen evidence of their trapping activities and would have to check their licenses.

The change in that place was like walking into the daylight after wandering for a long time in the dark. They laughed and produced their trapping and hunting licenses, which I found to be in order.

Then I said, "If you happen to have a drink around this place, I would certainly enjoy it."

One fellow ran and fetched a gallon of whiskey. Then they all had a good laugh and slapped me on the back.

My new friends wanted to know how I had discovered their hideaway, for I was the only person to have found it. They explained that they had their main cabin some two miles away, but had camouflaged this cabin by hiding it well in the bush while as a blind they had set traps along their access trails. I explained that but for my habit of cutting across country I would certainly never have found the place.

The market for their product was the loggers back in the bush who had to establish an alternative supply to avoid wandering in the desert of Prohibition.

That night we had a tremendous celebration, and the little cabin resounded with the laughter and song of some very relieved moonshiners. They persuaded me to stay over another day. My dogs were in need of some extra rest, but our little holiday ended the next morning. So ended my discovery of an illicit still, and I never ran into a whiskey cabin again.

From there I headed with some misgivings to Big River, for I had made all those enemies during the court cases on my last visit. To my astonishment, the people were friendly once again. Much to my relief, they appeared to have forgotten their hostility towards me. I was so happy finding people friendly and congenial again that I got to thinking it would be nice to leave the Department. I had been considering sending in my resignation for some time now, but I did not wish to let down Andy Holmes, who had remained my good friend. However, my chance came sooner than I expected.

At Big River, the local game guardian asked me to help him convict a fur buyer from Manitoba who was buying fur on a Manitoba license. Our man in Big River felt his witnesses would not be convincing enough for him to win the case or that no one would give evidence and the case would be dismissed. When I looked at the list of people who had sold fur to the buyer, I knew that one chap on the list would give evidence, for he was a friend of mine, though not a friend of our local man. It took me ten days to make a round trip fifteen miles beyond Green Lake to get him to come to court and testify.

I called Andy Holmes then and told him I had lost ten days but had produced a witness whose testimony had convinced the Justice of the Peace to levy a fine of twenty-five dollars. Holmes asked me to stay over for another day, as he would be coming to Big River by train the next day. So I lost one more day, and it was April and the snow was thawing.

When Holmes arrived, I realized at once that he was not pleased. "Why is it that it took the two of you game guardians to get evidence for something as minor as prosecuting a poor 'furlegger'?" he asked.

I gave him the long explanation that the witness was my friend but the local man's enemy, but he was not impressed. I was not happy about that particular visit with Andy Holmes.

The next morning I left for the Turtleford patrol, which led from Big River north and west to Green Lake, to Livelong, missing Meadow Lake by going thirty miles to the south, on to Turtleford and then to St. Walburg. I had the names of four persons from whom I was to get evidence of some game law infractions and to have them convicted.

When I got to Livelong, I mailed in my resignation, which would be effective at the end of May. It was then April 10, and the ground was partly bare. I was glad that I would be through with convictions, and could turn my life in another direction and see new places. The same patrols had grown wearisome.

I went to work, produced the evidence for the court cases and sent in my report on the matter. Andy Holmes was present at the trials, and we got our convictions. In the four years I had spent with the Department, I had had fifty-five cases where the accused were found guilty.

After the trials, Holmes and I had a good talk. He didn't want to accept my resignation. Instead he offered me a thirty-day holiday with pay to give me an opportunity to think things over. Paid holidays were very rare in those times, and I knew the offer was generous. My mind, however, was made up, and at last he accepted my resignation. Holmes really was a fine fellow and was convinced I was ready to go when I told him I had stayed so long in the service because of our friendship.

Trappers Harry Hughes and Hanson
(right) pose as mighty hunters for
the camera.

4

BEAR CUBS

I SPENT THE FALL OF 1925 in the harvest fields of southern Saskatchewan. It was a very satisfactory change for me to be rid of the responsibilities and regimentation of the Game Branch and to be once more close to the good land, gathering its produce, meeting new people, and making new friends.

There I met Vern Kingsberg and Ridge Brown, who hailed from Dundurn, Saskatchewan. They wanted to go to Little Bear Lake in the coming winter to do some commercial fishing and asked me to join them in a partnership. This was just made to order for me, and I accepted, while planning to do some trapping on the side to give me some extra income. It was generally known that commercial fishermen made poor wages by the time the net profits of a fishing season were allocated between the partners.

At that time, Little Bear Lake was an excellent source of lake trout. The lake had never been commercially fished to any extent before our arrival, and we were quite successful in our fishing venture as far as tonnage was concerned. The largest trout netted by our party weighed in at forty-three pounds dressed. We were able to get a team and sleigh in with our outfit and also used this mode of freighting to transport our fish to market in Prince Albert. However, our "net" profit was small.

For the balance of the winter, I went trapping with George Patterson, whom I had met earlier in the winter. We trapped the country between Big Sandy Lake (then known as Big Bear Lake) and Fishing Lakes in a country so beautiful that Fishing Lakes are now part of the Nipawin Provincial Park. We had a fair catch of lynx that winter, and we trapped muskrats on the Ballantyne River in the month of March, but the catch was small. In the spring Patterson left for Kinistino, Saskatchewan. I accompanied him as far as the White Fox River, where we spent a short time trapping muskrats, until Patterson decided to move on to Kinistino by way of Nipawin. I then began to pick up all my traps and prepared to walk overland to Prince Albert.

On my way westward the next day, I spotted two bear cubs climbing in a large spruce tree. Now, I knew that a market existed for live bear cubs and that if I could capture them unhurt I could increase my not-so-robust income for the season.

I would need help, what with the old mother bear probably lurking in the brush somewhere and the amazing agility of the cubs to consider. I had heard of a work crew cutting out the north boundary of the Fort-à-la-Corne Forest Preserve and knew they were not far from me because I had heard them chopping wood that morning. I walked about a mile to where I could hear someone felling a tree. From there, I soon located the camp and found the work crew.

I explained to these men that I needed their help to capture a couple of bear cubs. They were ready to accommodate me, since one of their number had shot the mother bear earlier in the day. They were now just going in for their supper and asked me to join them. I was in luck again, for no one was left out at mealtime.

The whole crew joined in the bear chase. One took an axe, and we all marched off to the site where I had last seen the bear cubs. They were on the ground when we arrived but scrambled up a tree at our arrival, not an ordinary tree but one of the tallest spruces I have ever seen. When the men cut down the tree, I grabbed one of the cubs and put it into a big burlap sack the men had given to me at the camp. The second cub was much more active and gave us the slip many times before we got it up a small tree, which we cut partly so that we could lower the cub gently to the ground. I reached up, took it by the neck and was able to put it into the bag after a brisk tussle, though it scratched my hands considerably before I could let go. However, I was happy that I was now the owner of two live and lively cubs. The men of the work crew wanted no part of my livestock. They had come along solely for the entertainment.

Now that I had the bears, I would have to feed and care for them until I could find a buyer. I had to find milk for the cubs. The site of their capture was south of where the town of Choiceland is today. At that time, there were only a few homesteaders moving into the area, but one day I had heard a cowbell some place back in the bush. Now, I struck out in the direction where I had heard this sound. I found a cabin in the dark and asked the man who answered my knock if he had any milk for sale. This man had no milking cattle, but he directed me to his nearby neighbour, who did possess a milch cow.

I came upon this man's place as he was about to enter his log cabin with an armful of wood. As it was very dark, I called out a greeting from a distance. At first he thought I was his neighbour, but I explained that I was a stranger, a trapper from the North with two small bear cubs in a sack and wondering if I might purchase some milk to feed them.

I can still see his reaction. He dropped his armful of stove wood and said, "I can get you some milk for the cubs, but where are you going and where will you stay for the night?"

"I'll camp in the bush somewhere," I replied.

"You are not going to camp in the bush," he said. "Come on into the house so my wife and I can see your bear cubs."

We introduced ourselves. They were Mr. and Mrs. Parker. Soon, they asked me if I had had my supper. When I told them I had some food with me, Mrs. Parker told me not to bother with that and proceeded to cook me a real meal. It was wonderful to meet such fine people and to receive such a warm welcome from absolute strangers. It was like meeting old friends. At that time I had no idea it was the beginning of a long and rewarding relationship with the Parkers. Starting the next winter, he would become my trapping partner.

While I was with the Parkers, the cubs were well fed and kept safe and sound in a wooden piano box. I returned to White Fox River for my tent and traps, for Parker would take me, my outfit and my bear cubs in his team and wagon as far as Henribourg, where he had to go to pick up a load of furniture shipped in from southern Saskatchewan, which had been his home before he came north.

It was the time of the spring thaw and flood, which meant hard travel for the horses. It took us two days to get to Henribourg, and the first night we camped in the vicinity of the present hamlet of Weirdale.

That morning I had no more milk for my growing and ever-hungry cubs. After we had travelled for a few miles, I saw five cows in a clearing and no buildings nearby. I got out my camping tea pail and went milking. A complete stranger to the cow that appeared most likely to give milk,

I approached her, hand held out, uttering what I hoped was friendly conversation. She tossed her head and moved away. As this situation called for some strategy, I returned to the wagon, where I talked to Parker. He took my tea pail and scooped some oats from the sack of oats he carried to keep his horses going.

"Try her with some oats," he said. "That way you can get better acquainted with Bossy and might get some results."

I must say that she appreciated the oats and willingly bartered her milk for them. As I walked off with the foamy white bear feed in my tin pail, I looked back at the cow and found that she was looking at me, so that I know we parted the best of friends. I have sometimes wondered what must have been the thoughts of the cow's owner at milking time, though I had taken only enough milk to tide the bears over until Henribourg, which we reached at about 3 P.M.

Here I hitched a ride to Prince Albert by car. I registered at the Prince Albert Hotel, which today is called the National Hotel. I asked Mr. Biggs, the hotelkeeper, if he had a place where I could keep the cubs for a couple of days.

Mr. Biggs was very accommodating. "Yes," he replied, "as long as you're registered at the hotel, you can keep the bears in our coal bin. It's been cleaned out and isn't in use in the summer. Provided you care for them yourself and clean up the bin when you leave, there will be no extra charge."

It was one of those instances of kindness and help that I received from friends, acquaintances, and even complete strangers in those times. I remarked to Parker when he came into town next day how lucky I had been to find a place to keep the cubs while I went looking for a buyer.

I then left for Saskatoon, for it was there I heard there was a market for live bear cubs. A dealer was buying them to fill an order for several small cubs. When I arrived, however, I was informed that the order had been filled.

As I left Prince Albert, Mr. Biggs had warned me he would feed the cubs only until the next day, and he expected me to be back then. I met his deadline, but when I walked into the lobby, he looked at me coldly and said, "You have a big bill to pay for the damage your baby bears have done to my coal bin."

I thought he was joking. "What can they damage in a room with concrete walls and floor?" I asked.

He then took me down to the coal bin so I could see the damage for myself. Much to my surprise, there was a steam heating pipe that came through the north wall near the cement floor and ran up the wall to the ceiling, then across the ceiling and out the south wall. The pipes had been covered with a heavy wrapping of insulation, and those pesky cubs had climbed up the pipe and across it many times, thereby tearing off all the insulation! It was a terrible mess.

I went over to see my old friend Mr. Van Ryswick at the confectionery to see if he could suggest someone who might want to buy the cubs. He could not help me in that respect, but he allowed me to keep the cubs temporarily in a shed at his place.

Finally I sold them for a song to Mr. F.F. Lund the taxidermist and creator of the Lund Wildlife Exhibit. Mr. Lund took his exhibit to fairs and exhibitions and used my cubs as a live exhibit to attract customers into his tent, where his mounted wild animals were on display. A leading attraction for several years, the cubs were kept in a unique cage built to closely resemble their natural habitat. Unpeeled poles were mounted as cage bars installed vertically to become realistic tree trunks. They were mounted into a heavy wooden floor, and the ceiling was made of the same plank-weight wood. The ceiling was camouflaged with green spruce boughs to top off the unique cage.

These bears could be observed by all and sundry at no charge. They were one black and one brown bear, and their antics were highly educational and entertaining to a great many people, particularly to school children, who had never seen live bears, and to almost everyone who had never been able to observe them at such close quarters. The highlight of their activities was the wrestling match they staged regularly and voluntarily. They were handsome beasts, well-fed and clean, and they seemed to be quite happy as they flung each other around the cage.

I have often wished, however, that I had left them to roam in the woods. It was another good experience from which I learned something. I am now in complete agreement with the advice to leave young bears and other baby wildlife where you see them alone in the bush. They are probably not orphans because the mother is usually nearby but out of sight.

I also agree with an old saying: "Give your enemy a bear cub or a buck deer fawn to raise as a pet. He is then certain to have a great deal of trouble."

There was one fringe benefit from this episode. Had it not been for the bear cubs, I would never have met Mr. and Mrs. Parker.

5

HARDSHIPS AND HAPPY DAYS

I N THE SUMMER OF 1926, I met William Tremblay. He was interested in doing some summer commercial fishing at Waskesiu Lake (then called Red Deer Lake). He asked me to join him and his brother George in this venture, and I was game to try commercial fishing as a summer occupation.

The Tremblay brothers built a boat and furnished the nets. I bought a Model T Ford car and converted it into a truck to haul in our outfit and to haul out our fish. After we had paid for groceries, a fishing license, gasoline for the first trip, and ice to preserve the catch, we had no money left for the license for the truck.

We decided to leave Prince Albert very early the next morning on our way to Waskesiu, so we would be less likely to meet anyone on the road with authority to stop us and enquire about our non-existent license plates. Unfortunately the road was wet and we were delayed several times because we got stuck in the mudholes caused by recent heavy rains. Just as we got underway after lunch, we met Constable Powers of the Saskatchewan Provincial Police on his way to Prince Albert from Lac La Ronge. Of course he halted us and asked us about the missing license plates.

After a few years in the bush, Hanson was adept at hunting for big game to feed all mouths at camp.

I had to do some fast thinking. I explained to the police officer that I had just bought the truck with a small down payment so I could try it out for one trip to see if it operated to my satisfaction.

He wanted to know the name of the party from whom I had obtained the truck and if I intended to complete the deal. I replied that the truck seemed to be functioning satisfactorily and I named the firm. I promised to buy a license as soon as we had unloaded at Waskesiu Lake and returned to Prince Albert. Much to my surprise, Powers let me proceed after giving me a stern warning that I comply with my promise and be sure to advise the dealer that he should have hung a dealer's license plate on the truck before releasing it to me.

My luck continued to hold out, for we arrived safely over a very substandard road. We caught a load of fish in short order for the return trip. Thereafter, I drove with the truck properly licensed, as evidenced by my spanking new license plates.

We occupied ourselves with summer fishing until harvest time. Then I accompanied the Tremblay brothers to Davidson, Saskatchewan, where I worked for Herb Brooks. Harvesting was always a welcome change for me because I met and worked with many different people and always made new friends. Besides, it was a sure method of obtaining a grubstake for my trapping activities in the great North Country.

After harvest I met a young man named Herman Mosher, who wanted to learn the trapping business from me. In spite of the fact I told him I had promised to trap with another man that winter, I took him with me, for I did not know whether Parker might have changed his mind. When we arrived at his homestead, however, he was ready to go. I told him there would be three of us going, to which he readily agreed, saying that with three of us he could come home occasionally in the winter.

On the day preceding the opening of the trapping season, the three of us arrived at an old trapping cabin in the area I had trapped with George Patterson. We had four dogs and a well-loaded toboggan. Then we worked long days cutting firewood, making temporary repairs to the old cabin which would house us until we could build a new one, cutting logs, training dogs, setting traps, and hunting for meat to feed ourselves and our dog team. On the second day after our arrival, I solved the meat problem by shooting a moose.

Our appetites grew with the passing days, so that one quarter of a moose seemed to be consumed in no time at all. Parker observed one day that soon the three of us would be eating a quarter of a moose a day, but of course it could not come to that. Certainly we had all become great eaters as a result of all our outdoor activity in the growing cold of late autumn.

To start things off, we had good luck on the trapline. By the time we had completed the new cabin, we had also caught seven red foxes, one cross fox, and one fisher.

We had cached one hundred pounds of flour and fifty pounds of sugar at a place about fifteen miles south of our camp. We had left it there at the end of the cut road when our outfit was freighted in that far with a team of horses. One day Mosher and Parker decided to take the dog team to freight in these supplies to our present camp. I would stay home to chink the walls of the new cabin with sphagnum moss by pounding it in between the logs. Also, in their absence, I would move all our effects into the new cabin from the old dilapidated structure that we had been using, and which stood a stone's throw away from the new one.

In the old cabin, we had an ancient cast iron wood-burning stove, which Patterson and I had freighted from Little Bear Lake in the previous winter. It had two lids on top; the firebox was three feet in long, and it kept fire all night. Before Mosher and Parker left that morning, I had them shake out the coals from last night's fire and carry the heavy stove over to the new cabin.

As my partners left, I had been busy cutting wood and carrying in frozen moss to thaw out. After about two hours of hammering moss well into the cracks between the logs that made up the walls, I heard a shot, then several more in rapid and scattered fire. As I hurried to see what was going on, I thought it sounded like some kind of warfare. When I got out, I saw the old cabin all ablaze.

I ran over and saved my .22 rifle and my big game rifle with five cartridges in its magazine. They were standing outside, leaning against a wall. I also got the fisher pelt, skinned but not yet stretched, from where it hung on a nail in the outside wall, also a quarter of a moose left hanging there. I could see the meat grinder through the flames crackling about the open doorway. I bolted over to the new cabin, seized my axe, cut a long pole just before the roof fell in. This was the total extent of the salvage.

After the cabin had totally burned down, I realized I had no food except the piece of moose meat. Carrying only my rifle and hunting knife, which was always at my belt and therefore not in the burnt cabin, I struck off down the trail to follow my partners on the fifteen mile walk to Caribou Creek, where I knew they would be camped for the night.

When I found them, they had made camp and had a good fire going in the gathering dusk of a day in early winter. Before they recovered from their surprise at my arrival, I asked them if they had anything to eat. They indicated that they had one bannock, half a tin of honey and a little moose meat.

"Well," I said, "I would certainly appreciate having some of that, since the last meal I've had was at breakfast with you fellows, and there's no more food at the cabin."

Then I explained exactly what had happened. In the moving of the stove, somehow a live coal had fallen out unnoticed. Whether it fell inside or outside the cabin was not important, for that coal had smouldered in combustible material until it had burst into flame and climbed up the wall. I named the few articles I had saved, along with the few tools that I had been working with at the new cabin. Then there were those articles that Mosher and Parker had taken with them, the dogs and the toboggan and the sugar and flour at this end. All else was gone.

This loss was not welcome what with winter having just arrived. That night, as we sat around the campfire, I glanced at Parker and then at Herman Mosher. Mosher was barely out of his teens, and he was taking our loss very hard; he seemed about to burst into tears. Two big game rifles and a .22 rifle had burned; for some reason my partners had taken neither along that morning. Also gone were all our hard-earned fox furs and all our food, clothes and bedding, right down to personal articles in the cabin.

Parker had been observing the situation. He was not a man to be thwarted for any length of time by adversity. He looked at me and grinned; then he started to chuckle, and finally he was laughing.

"Mosher," he said, "there is nothing to worry about. We are all in good health, and we have our strength. All we need to do is make different plans."

That put Mosher in a brighter mood right away. It was great to have a guy like Parker around.

We took turns that night sleeping in the one sleeping bag. We also took turns at keeping the fire going, so that we spent a reasonably comfortable night.

The next day, Mosher and I walked back to camp, while Parker turned south with the dog team towards Torch River, where Tom Brothers had a trapping cabin. We had good fortune there, for these gentlemen loaned us a good load of groceries and some spare bedding.

Every time Parker went out that winter, to his home or to White Fox or Nipawin, he brought in supplies, so that even with our hard luck we spent a good winter.

Fur prices were very good. A fine dark fisher pelt, for example, would bring as much as one hundred and twenty dollars.

There were only a few fisher in the country. Any time we saw their tracks, we knew they had been made by a lone animal travelling through trapping territory and that it would not return.

One day I decided to follow one when I saw its fresh tracks in the deep snow where it had cut across my trapline. It was evening when I discovered this sign, and I hit the trail early next morning. I took two traps, my .22 rifle and enough food to last for three days. I began to trail the fisher, tracking it for a long time until I saw where it had bolted as I got quite close. Spurred on by the realization that my quarry carried a hundred-dollar pelt, I tracked and trailed until darkness forced me to make camp.

I made my usual fire, about seven feet long, and built my usual type of shelter for camping out without my bedroll—a mat of spruce boughs thick enough to keep me out of the snow while I lay or sat by the fire. After I cut a supply of wood and melted snow to make coffee, I spent a fairly good night by taking naps of from one to three hours before awakening to tend the fire. Then I would have another cup of coffee and a snack before I fell asleep again, keeping up this routine until daybreak.

This was my first attempt at walking down a fisher; therefore, I did not know what to expect. I was off as soon as it was light enough to travel, and I kept to one side of its trail. For half an hour I saw no tracks; then I came upon its track again. I stayed on the trail then for three hours. When it led to the edge of an open muskeg, I saw the fisher for the first time. It was crossing the width of the muskeg now and showed up as a dark moving object against the snow. I increased my walking speed, knowing that I was getting very close. The fisher tried to throw me off the trail by following rabbit trails, so I lost valuable time searching out the tracks and allowing the fisher some time to rest. I saw it twice more that day, but it kept to the thick forest. I had been very close to it at the last sighting. Darkness overtook me again, and once more I made a lonely camp by the fire and huddled on my spruce bough bed. I was almost certain that I would get a shot at that fisher some time the next day.

I had been trailing the fisher for some three hours the next morning when I found it had entered an old fox den, a hole in the ground on a small knoll in sparsely treed country. I scraped away the deep snow and began to dig using the only method I had—using my axe to chop at the frozen ground. I soon gave up on this activity and began to think instead. I set my two traps in the hole. Then I went into the bush and cut a birch sapling about one and one half inches in diameter and about ten feet long. I made a lunch then to see if the fisher would come out of the hole, but of course it did not. After my lunch and coffee, I pushed the birch sapling down into the hole until all ten feet had been forced into the den. Then I saw the fisher's head as it almost popped out of the hole. I stopped moving the stick and pushed the two set traps down as far as I could reach, past where I had last seen the fisher. Then I began to move the birch sapling. It was only a few moments before I heard the trap snap and the fisher came bounding out of the hole, fighting the trap clamped on its fore paw. For a moment it did not notice me, during which time I shot it through the head.

I got back to camp after midnight. I was fortunate that it was a clear night and I could use the stars as a guide as I struck out across country—a much shorter and more direct route than backtracking along the erratic trail the fisher had chosen to make for me. Had it been cloudy, I would have spent another night by the campfire, huddled against the cold.

Later that winter, that particular fisher brought us eighty dollars.

My next attempt to walk down a fisher occurred one day when Parker and I were setting snares and traps for a lynx. We had left our Springs Camp in the Narrow Hills and were working our way to the next camp about twenty-five miles away. As it began to grow dark and we were only about a mile from this camp, we noticed the fresh track of a fisher where it had crossed our trail.

That night the weather turned very cold. In the morning, I told Parker to stay in camp while I would go after the fisher. He tried to make me change my mind, but I was confident that I could play it out and shoot it or get it to go into a den. Parker, I know, did not want to see me camping out alone in the tremendous cold of a northern midwinter.

At daybreak, I went back to where I had seen the fisher track. I had donned my snowshoes, and with two traps and a light packsack containing some grub, I set out tracking my quarry. After about fifteen minutes of walking, I found the tracks leading into a hole in the ground and no tracks leading away from it. Once again I cleared away the snow and began to dig with my belt axe. The ground was so gravelly I knew I could seriously damage the axe blade, so I quit digging. I set the traps in the tunnel and went back to camp. When I told Parker I had a fisher boxed up in a hole he just looked at me and scratched his head.

We had a good lunch, took a big axe and two of our sleigh dogs, and returned to the hole. The fisher had not been caught in either trap. We had just started to dig when one of the dogs began digging at a spot about seven feet to one side of where we were at work. When I investigated, I found another hole slanting downward toward where we were working. The other dog got into the act by digging furiously at the first hole and barking with excitement. The two holes were about six feet apart. I cut a willow a bit longer than that, called off the dogs and set the two traps at the entrance of one hole. Manipulating the willow from the other end, I must have prodded the fisher, for I heard a trap snap shut as he suddenly burst from the hole on the other side. We had our fisher, a prize winner, jet black in colour.

The darker a fisher pelt, the better the price, and we realized one hundred and two dollars and fifty cents for this one. We also picked up a lynx on this trip, so it turned out to be what trappers consider a good trapline patrol.

When I attempted to walk down my third fisher that winter, I experimented to see if there was an easier way. When I found its track, I made the usual preparations. I put on my snowshoes and took along a dog to help me run down the fisher when I got close enough. By now I was confident that I could do it.

But I learned another lesson. In less than two days, the dog was unable to keep up the pace. He played out as he broke through the soft snow, while I did not sink more than three or four inches on my snowshoes. It was in the open muskeg that the dog took most of the punishment. He floundered, while I made steady progress.

That fisher hunt ended in failure. I had to strike out for our nearest trapline trail, which was less than three miles away, to find solid footing for my dog. Then I had to tie a line around his neck and lead him home, so that he would not be accidentally caught in one of our traps. We arrived at camp after dark. That was the first and last time I ever took a dog to help me track down a fisher.

Our fisher catch that winter totalled three. Mosher had caught the first when it had been trapped accidentally in a weasel set. Then there were the two I had tracked down.

Parker continued to make freighting trips that winter to bring in groceries and essential equipment. He made the last trip of the season at the end of March, some seventy miles to Joe Blair's store a little west of where the village of Love is today—it was then called Love Siding. At that time of the year, it was a little too risky to cross the Saskatchewan River on the ice to go to nearby Nipawin, a much larger trading centre, for there was as yet no bridge there and ferry service only in summer.

Parker then left for the season, returning to his homestead some time in early April. Mosher and I planned to stay on until mid-May to trap beaver and muskrat. Although we were in rather poor muskrat country, we ended the season with ninety-seven muskrats and eleven beaver pelts.

We began to run out of flour near the end of April. With only five pounds left, we took three pounds with us when we made a side trip to McDougal Creek to trap beaver. We planned on eating this flour with the meat of the beavers and muskrats we would trap. We ranged almost to Big Sandy Lake on this particular jaunt, returning some days later to our base tent in a state of semi-starvation. We had been thinking of the bit of flour we had left there—enough for two bannocks—and of how good that would taste. Even before we reached the tent, I was aware that we had had a visitor for I could see daylight through the tent from end to end.

A bear had pulled down everything we had left hanging from the ridgepole, and our flour was scattered from the tent all the way to the riverbank. There would be no bannock for us that night, so we had to make a meal from the carcass of a beaver which we had brought with us from the trapline. The only damage to the tent was a big rip in the back where friend bear had made his exit.

Next day, we pulled up our traps and called it quits for another season. We headed for the main cabin, where a stay of two days would be required to stretch and dry our furs before we trekked on foot the seventy long miles to the Parker homestead, a trail that would lead us some distance south of Choiceland. One more beaver was our reward when we pulled up our traps, and we would rely on its meat and the two pounds of flour we had left in the main camp to see us through as food until we arrived at Parker's.

On our way to the main camp we were both carrying bulging pack-sacks. I stopped and cached all the traps, as they were just too heavy to carry. They could be picked up next season. Now we had seven miles of open muskeg to wade through. The spring thaw had melted all the snow so that we trudged along in the bog, which was brimming with icy cold water. We staggered into the camp about 4 P.M. Pancakes were going to be a great treat this evening.

As soon as I opened the door, I saw a beaver trap and a note lying on the table. "I found your trap with a beaver in it," I read. "As you told me

I could have the beaver, I have brought you the trap. I caught only one more beaver and fourteen muskrats this spring. I went upriver until I found one of your sets. As I have been on short rations, I helped myself to your flour and made one small bannock, as I see you have so little here. I hope you have more at your other camp anyway. I did not take near half the flour. I still have some smoked caribou for a few snacks along the road. Thanks for the beaver. Your friend, Eldon Lockhart."

After I read the note I looked at the flour sack. It contained only enough to make two good-sized pancakes, so we decided to save it for our forced march. However, after looking through everything, I came up with about a cupful of pot barley. We felt very good about that. I boiled the barley until it was cooked, then dumped it into the frying pan with some moose tallow and fried some beaver meat to go with it. This description may suggest a poor meal to some, but in reality it was wonderful how good it tasted to us. When you are really hungry, anything edible tastes good. We enjoyed that meal as much as if we had been eating T-bone steak with all the trimmings plus dessert.

That night passed while we were both in a dead sleep.

When I awoke in the morning, I had a good deal of pain in my back and chest. I guessed that this condition had resulted from our wading in ice cold water all the previous day while crossing that big open muskeg. Only by leaning with my back firmly pressed against the cabin wall and drawing only half a breath could I escape the pain.

It took us three days to stretch and dry our beaver pelts. During this time, we lived on beaver meat only, still saving our bit of remaining flour for the long trek to Parker's place. On the afternoon of the third day, we set out, carefully tucking our meagre quantity of flour, now in the form of two pancakes, into my packsack. My chest and back were still very sore, and I could not draw a full breath. This convinced me that I could not travel very fast with my packsack and load weighing sixty-five pounds, the same weight as Mosher was carrying.

We walked until midnight, having taken a rest every three or four miles. Then we hit the trail again, and it might have been 3 or 4 A.M. when we stopped and ate one half of a pancake each and washed it down with a little coffee that we had been saving for this trip. My painful condition was not improving, but we spread our bedrolls and had a good sleep in the moderate weather of spring in northern Saskatchewan.

We got underway again at about 9 A.M. As I rolled up my bedroll,

I became aware that the pain in my back was worse, but when I shouldered my packsack and eased into the shoulder straps, the weight of the pack against my back relieved the discomfort slightly.

After walking a few miles, I came upon a spruce hen sitting on a limb of a nearby spruce tree. I stopped and said to Mosher, "There's our dinner, Herman."

He shot it with the .22 rifle he was carrying. We walked on until we came to a flowing stream where we plucked and cooked that chicken. Needless to say, there were no edible parts wasted. When we left that place, we still had a few spoonfuls of moose tallow and one pancake. That was all we had remaining in the way of a food supply.

Early in the afternoon, we crossed the Torch River, where we ate the pancake, our last morsel of food, unless you count the bit of moose tallow. It was still twenty miles to the Parker farm. We followed the Fort-à-la-Corne Road all the way to Bissett Creek. Then I knew we had eight miles left to our destination. I asked Mosher how he felt.

"My legs are funny," he said. "There's almost no feeling in them."

"I'm going to cache the packsacks," I told him. "It's getting too late now for us to make it to Parker's if we carry all this weight."

I cut a big blaze on a tree, took sixty paces away from this tree and at right angles to the road, and hung the packsacks high in a spruce tree, where they could not be seen from the road.

Now our course led south-eastward through the forest. My back, released from the weight of my packsack became much more painful, and taking of a full breath was out of the question. I therefore pressed my back hard against a tree every time the pan became unbearable. These forced stops came at intervals of about fifteen minutes.

We arrived at 11 P.M. to find the Parkers abed. Parker promised right off to ride for our packs first thing in the morning to retrieve them via pony and packsaddle. He could see that we were in bad shape, both played out and I hampered by my sore back. Mrs. Parker arose from her bed and at once set about to make us a good supper, but I warned her that we had better eat lightly, for we had gradually lost our food intake and might become violently ill if we ate our fill. She then served us each a sandwich, coffee, and a glass of fresh country cow's milk. Parker, good fellow that he was, poured us a stiff drink of whiskey. For a while I felt very little pain, but when I awoke next morning I could still not breathe properly.

Parker left long before I awoke and was back with the packsacks in time for the noon meal. Meanwhile, I kept warning Mosher not to eat too much but to increase his food intake slightly with each meal. We rested and were served well by the Parkers for the next two days.

Then it was on to Nipawin. On our way we stopped at Joe Blair's store near Love Siding where we had our fur account. Our returns awaited us there from a previous shipment, and Blair advanced us a goodly sum on the current one.

At Nipawin, Parker asked me if I thought we could eat normally, and I judged it was now safe to do so. My chest pains had also subsided somewhat. For starters, we registered at a hotel and brought up a case of beer to the room. We had two bottles of beer each to whet even more our ravenous appetites, then went to a Chinese restaurant to see what they were offering on their menu.

Our first meal was a regular T-bone steak and French fries. After I had eaten it, I felt that I could eat another. So we ordered another meal of T-bone steaks and fried mushrooms all around. The first meal had been on Parker, the second on me, so now Mosher asked if we could eat another meal. I answered that I could, but it would have to be something other than T-bone steak. I asked Parker if he was game. He must have been thinking about the short rations we had endured after the disastrous fire that had burned all our food that winter, and about our forced march on next to nothing to eat. A big eater any time, he said it all when he replied with a bit of a flourish, "Gentlemen, we are here to celebrate."

We ordered a round of pork and beans. The waitress began to walk away in disbelief, but we finally persuaded her that we were serious. I recall that I did not feel too good for a short time after eating the last order, but Parker and Mosher were enjoying everything.

My sore chest was improving. After a couple of hours and another beer we returned to the same restaurant. If the members of the staff were amazed at us tucking away three dinners at one sitting, they were absolutely dumfounded when we ordered three banana splits each.

So ended our celebration of a season of hardship, good trapping and, probably most rewarding, good fellowship. Then we parted company. Parker returned to his farm, later became a forest ranger, and then farmed again until he passed away. Mrs. Parker is still living with her son, who farms near Choiceland.

Mosher and I went to Prince Albert, where we purchased a seven-passenger Studebaker car and a taxi license. Mosher took a job at the Prince Albert Hotel, while I drove the taxi. We sold out at the end of the summer and went off to work on the gathering of the year's harvest.

When it was all gathered in, Herman Mosher decided to go home to Prince Edward Island. "I read in the Charlottetown newspaper," he said to me, "that a fellow and his companion walked forty miles in one day. I'll show them on the Island that I can walk clean around the damned thing in a day."

I never heard from him again.

6

COMMERCIAL FISHERMAN

I T WAS IN THE FALL OF 1927 that I joined in a partnership to go trapping with William Osmund of Kinistino, Saskatchewan, who furnished the dog team and the toboggan. Osmund was with me until April of 1928, when he took the dogs out to civilization before the snow melt.

About that time I was joined by Kai Thorson, who worked with me during spring trapping. On May 17, Thorson and I left the main camp and walked (on full rations) all the way to Nipawin by way of Joe Blair's store to have our fur shipped out to be sold.

Although the trapping season had been a success financially, we arrived in Nipawin with one dollar between us, all the cash we had. Osmund was in Kinistino with all the money for our winter fur catch, and we had not taken an advance from Blair for our fur delivery to him. We would have to wait until the returns came back from the fur auction in Winnipeg. Thorson and I spent our cash on a telephone call to Osmund, but were told that he was away on a visit and would not be home for three or four days. No telephone existed in the place he was visiting, so for the moment we were dead broke.

Neither of us knew any of the businessmen in Nipawin, but it was essential that we find room and board and a change of clothes. Fortunately, I had no difficulty in obtaining board and room for both of us with no down payment. Now to see about the new clothing.

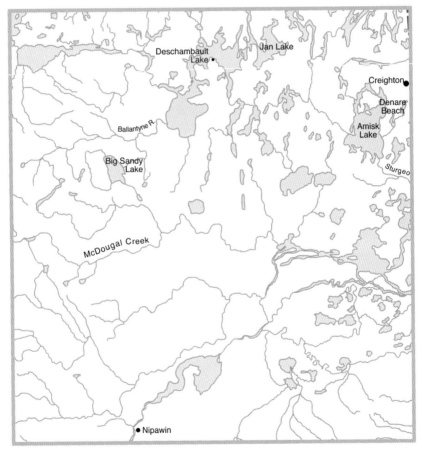

Before fishing commercially on these
northern lakes, Hanson and crew had to
clear roads through the bush to freight
their supplies in and their catch out
to Nipawin.

After dinner we walked down the street. Thorson turned to me, "We look more like bums than anything else," he muttered as we stopped and sized up the tattered and soiled rags we were wearing. "I don't think anyone will trust us," he added.

"Where there is a will there is a way," I recited the old platitude without much conviction, I am afraid. I stood reading the names on the store fronts until farther down the street there appeared a sign "Smith & Kent." I got up my nerve and went in. When the girl behind the counter looked at me, I asked if I might speak to the manager. She pointed to a little office in one corner of the building.

As I came to his door the manager looked up from his work. I introduced myself and gave him the facts. He gave me a very steady look for a moment before he replied, "How much credit do you need, Mr. Hanson?"

When I indicated that the amount would be under twenty dollars, he quickly rose and served me himself in the amount of seventeen dollars worth of clothing. When I came out of the store, Thorson was waiting for me, but when he saw the parcel under my arm he said, "Olaf, I just don't have the nerve to do that."

Later that day I borrowed five dollars from the keeper of the rooming house where we were staying. With this money we each got a haircut and enough beer to celebrate the end of our trapping season.

Osmund arrived sooner than we had expected—two days later, with the money. I went to Smith & Kent's store and paid my bill. The manager was mildly surprised that I was paying so soon, as I had said it would be a week. I asked him if he expected I would ever pay him, but he only shrugged and said he had not doubted my word from the beginning.

We all left for Prince Albert in Bill Osmund's car. Later that summer, Thorson and I went out to the Torch River Settlement, a district north of Love Siding. We filed on homesteads and spent the summer there clearing enough land to meet the terms of our homesteaders' obligations. Osmund, meanwhile, had gotten married to a very nice girl and quit trapping. That fall I spent the harvest season at Codette, just south of Nipawin.

After harvest I invested in five sleigh dogs. Four of them were half-husky, from the same litter. The fifth was part wolfhound, and I eventually rid myself of it, for it did not have the heart of the others and so did not work well with the team. The remaining four became the best pulling unit I ever owned. They could haul a full load all day, and I rode on the toboggan part of the time.

Kai Thorson was my partner again that fall. We headed for the same location as our previous season, our main cabin at Springs Camp. The camp was in the bush, away from any lake or river, but only about fifteen feet from an excellent fresh-water spring. From the cabin we could hear the water cascading over the small dam we had built to create a catch basin. Here one could dip a pail of clear water on any day of the year. Even in midwinter temperatures of −50 or −60°F, we could dip a full pail. Looking back to those days I realize it was that spring and its excellent water that made me return to this same location for several years. The wonderfully clear and good-tasting water was so attractive that I drank more water while I was there than at any other place I have lived. I believe it had a lot to do with keeping me in robust health.

That winter fur animals were not plentiful, so we finished the season making modest wages. Even the small gold mine I once thought I had found in walking down fishers failed me, as I tracked down only one more after that winter with Parker and Mosher. Besides, fishers had become very scarce, and the price on their pelts had dropped considerably.

In the spring we came back to our homesteads at Torch River Settlement. Our homesteads adjoined, and we helped each other build cabins. I did not quite finish mine, for in that summer of 1929 there were many bush fires, and we joined the fire-fighters.

After harvest I had a discussion with Robertson and Dainard, who were in a business partnership. They were interested in getting a bush road cut to Fishing Lakes to be able to freight out winter-caught fish. I suggested we might have better luck if we cut a road into Big Sandy Lake, a considerable distance farther north, where I knew the fishing was better but so far considered out of reach for commercial fishing. They balked at this idea, but when I explained that there were old roads leading to the region they went along with my suggestion.

It would be about one hundred miles by this road from Nipawin to Big Sandy Lake. However, there was a cut road to McDougal Creek, and from there we could follow an old Canadian Pacific survey line and a trapline that crossed a good deal of open muskeg all the way to Big Sandy Lake.

Robertson supplied the fishing outfit, which included about thirty nets, and Dainard financed the groceries. I was responsible for recruiting a crew. I took on a partner by the name of Klaus Vanema, who was a Torch River homesteader. He sank four hundred dollars into the venture. I also hired two fellows who had been harvesting with me and two experienced northern fishermen who had worked out of Big River. Alex

Chisholm, a Nipawin farmer, would freight out the fish. He also hauled up a load of supplies before freeze-up. Following the old roads, he made it almost to Big Sandy Lake with team and wagon, on a solid road base along what is known as the Narrow Hills. The Narrow Hills are in reality a giant esker that looks like a continuous abandoned railway embankment, overgrown with trees. It runs generally northward for many miles. From there, Chisholm gained access to an old road known as the Hudson Pacific Team Road, which had been cut from Prince Albert in 1916 while cutting out baselines. It ended in a swamp not far from Big Sandy Lake. Four of our men had widened and cleared this unused roadway so that Chisholm could get his team through.

Klaus Vanema and I built a camp on an island in Big Sandy Lake and cut out the road to the point Chisholm had reached earlier, to complete the road all the way to Nipawin.

It was the first time that Big Sandy Lake had been fished commercially. The fishing was so good that in the beginning we were getting an average of fifty whitefish to the net, which we set overnight. Ten days after the fishing season had opened, we had caught enough fish to recover our cash outlay, and by Christmas we were making money and paying wages to the men. We had also paid for all of our equipment. However, by now the fish catch had dropped off to ten fish per net, a fact that points up the fragility of the ecology of this region. Lakes have been fished out many times in northern waters, where fish growth is hampered by absence of enough fish food and by the long freeze-up season, with the result that sunlight is scanty and fish growth slow. At this time, fish prices had also fallen discouragingly.

I decided to cut a road to Ballantyne Bay on Deschambault Lake so that we would have an access road there for future fishing operations, and also do some fishing there to round out our activities in the present fishing season. We completed the road without much trouble because we followed on the ice of the Ballantyne River a good deal of the way. Another great help was the fact that it was late winter, and all the swamps we had to cross were solidly frozen at this time of the year.

When one of the freighters came into Big Sandy Lake to haul out the last of the fish, we had him haul our nets and outfit to Ballantyne Bay, where I had repaired an old abandoned cabin for a new headquarters. When he returned, this freighter took one load of fish out from Ballantyne Bay, as we had set out several nets and the fishing was very good.

From there we moved on to the Deschambault Lake Settlement. We were making good catches and had two loads ready to be freighted to Nipawin when a trapper arrived from Pelican Narrows with a message for me. Robertson and Dainard had sent the following message: "Stop fishing. The bottom has fallen out of the fish market."

We sold some of our fish to the natives for any price—they could use it for dog food—and we gave the rest away. Then we built a large wooden box and covered it with galvanized iron. In this box, we packed our fishnets to guarantee that they would remain dry. Fish nets were woven from linen in those days and would rot if they weren't cared for properly.

There were only three of us left when we started our long walk to the Torch River Settlement. As we moved south, I blazed a road in high country to be cut out next season for our return. The original road on the Ballantyne River and across the bogs would not be frozen hard enough for team traffic at the time we intended to return to Deschambault Lake next season.

When we arrived at our homesteads, we found that thanks to the arrival of the Great Depression there was very little work, and for the moment we were unemployed. We did manage to get on with a work crew building roads for a short time, and then we went fighting bush fires. When the harvest started in 1930, grain prices were so low that harvesters' wages had dropped by fifty per cent. Together with a very wet fall, our financial future seemed very bleak indeed.

At that time I met Chris Walker, a farmer from Pontrilas, Saskatchewan. When I was stooking for him out in the field one day, I told him that after harvest I would be going to Deschambault Lake to do some commercial fishing. Walker wanted to do the freighting for me, and so began an association that lasted for several seasons, until I gave up commercial fishing for good in that part of Saskatchewan.

From the nearby village of Armley, Walker found an experienced fisherman named Bob Fred who was willing to join us. Fred was something of a go-getter and arranged to meet us at the fishing camp on Deschambault Lake. He hired a teamster to take him to a spot near Big Sandy Lake, then he would continue on foot. Before leaving the teamster, Fred advised him to be at Deschambault Lake by December 8 to pick up four loads of fish that he would have ready to go. I had given him the key to our box of nets so that he could start as soon the season opened.

Meanwhile I had hired my neighbour Zack Anderson to haul in some of our freight. He had a team of light horses, which I thought would have less trouble in the soft places in the road where a heavier team might get bogged down.

A three-day snowstorm that began on October 15, 1930 had left two feet of snow covering everything and insulating the unfrozen swamps so that the frost did not penetrate to freeze things up for good travelling. It was so bad in fact that my neighbour Klaus Vanema expressed grave doubts that we could get through. I replied that we had no other choice if we wanted to make a living that winter. On this trip we were accompanied by one other member from the crew of the previous year.

By walking ahead of the team and packing down the snow with our snowshoes, we arrived at McDougal Creek in two days of travel. We built a cabin and a stable to hold four teams of horses. Here Anderson left us to return home and bring up a load of supplies and feed for his horses. Two of us went ahead now on the trail to Deschambault Lake tramping down the snow as we went, as this area is largely floating bog. Compacting the snow causes it to lose its insulating qualities so the frost can penetrate downward, thus permitting a team to travel.

We were now halfway to Ballantyne River from our McDougal Creek base. Anderson was busy freighting up supplies in relays. We worked our way steadily northward, across Mossy River, past the turn to Big Sandy Lake and down an old survey trail, where we cut out the old high stumps which signified that a horse team had never travelled here before. We crossed Herman Lake on twelve inches of ice. This lake is named for Herman Ehrlich, an old timer in the North.

On December 3, we struck Ballantyne River. I had ordered the fish haulers in by December 5, saying there would be two loads ready to go by that date.

The road I had blazed southward in the previous spring still had to be cut out, and we got at the job early the next day. When we returned after dark to the base camp we were using at the time, we found that Chris Walker had arrived with two teams. I had not expected him that early. The next day, five of us were cutting road when two passing Indians stopped by and agreed to help. With seven men cutting, we moved right along, but the heavier of the horses were still getting bogged down from time to time, and of course the freighters were getting worried.

The next night Mr. Jardine caught up to us with two more teams that belonged to Walker. Counting Anderson's horses, there were now five teams in camp and feed was getting scarce. There was not enough time now to tramp the open bog and let it freeze overnight. In the worst places we had horses walking on makeshift corduroy.

By December 6 some of the teamsters declared that they had had enough and were ready to return home. To encourage them to stay on the job I said, "Boys, it's only about a mile to Ballantyne Bay from here."

It was a clear moonlit night, and two of us walked ahead, to locate the road. We were on a narrow ridge with solid footing. After only a few hundred feet we found that we were on the road cut from Big Sandy Lake to Ballantyne Bay in the previous winter. Our ice testing showed that the ice on the lake was from fourteen to sixteen inches thick.

Back with the teamsters I gave them the good news. We celebrated by making a belated lunch. The teamsters, heartened by the good news, cut out the balance of the road that night and drove the sleighs to the shore of Ballantyne Bay, where they arrived at 10 P.M.

We followed the shore for about five miles to Bear Point, where we had left our cook stove with a native fellow named Noah Ballantyne. He lived at this place in winter time, making it a base for his trapping operations. There was an old vacant log cabin here for our use, and while our two native road cutters, Adam Roberts and Adam Ballantyne, cut some firewood, at about 1 A.M. I got out the griddle and began to fry pancakes. We were all very hungry, so I kept making pancakes and frying bacon and set out syrup and jam, of which we had a good supply. It was near 5 A.M. by the time we all had our fill and spread our sleeping bags on the floor.

By noon on the next day, all teams were travelling on the ice. The going was fine until we reached the narrows leading from Ballantyne Bay to Deschambault Lake.

Here we encountered dangerous ice conditions. A pressure ridge several feet high that was strung out from shore to shore barred our progress. We passed the danger by trekking around it on shore and skirting this obstacle from a safe distance.

Later that afternoon, we came to yet more dangerous ice. It was so thin that we decided to head for shore and make camp while some of the men went ahead testing the ice so as not to the horses into the lake. Following close to shore, we found thicker ice, so that on December 8 we reached Deschambault Lake Settlement.

My man from Armley who had preceded us earlier in the season was to be on the lake by this time with four loads of fish ready to be hauled back. We had also sent Klaus Vanema ahead to help him. When I asked the native people at the settlement if they had caught lots of fish, they pointed to the cabin where they were staying and to two men fishing out in the distance on the ice. They had big piles of fish, I was told.

We had a hard time getting past the settlement on account of very thin ice. The freighters declared they would not return this way with loaded sleighs. This meant that I must plan on cutting a portage around the settlement for their return trip. Finally we made it to Tower Island and our fishing camp.

Our men, Klaus Vanema and Bob Fred from Armley, were astonished to see us. As they had walked across country from Big Sandy Lake to Ballantyne River, they were walking in water in the floating bogs; therefore, they did not think it possible for the horses to get through at this time. As a result, they had been in no hurry to start fishing, had set only four nets and hadn't even bothered to fit the other nets with floats and sinkers. At present they had only one and a half loads of fish ready to go.

This was a great disappointment to the freighters, for they had only enough hay to last the horses for two days. Anderson left next morning for Bear Pont, where Noah Ballantyne had cut a large quantity of hay with a scythe for the pony he used to pull his toboggan on the trapline. He obtained enough hay to last our teams for eight or nine days. When our freighters were able to haul in supplies on their next trip from Nipawin, they were able to replace the hay.

Now everyone concentrated on fishing. In two days, Jardine's loads were sent out, and five days later Walker left with his loads. Walker would come back in two weeks, or about the end of December. Next morning we had the fifth load ready for Anderson, the last teamster to leave. Meanwhile some of the crew had built a horse barn and had cut logs for a new camp. We had done rather well.

A week later another fishing outfit pulled in. The word was getting around that there was now an open road to Deschambault Lake. We immediately made a deal with them. I loaned their teamster a load of fish to take back, while they helped us build our new camp. Then we helped them set their nets. When their teamster returned for the second load, they were all staying at our camp. They later returned our load of fish.

When Walker returned, we still had more fish than he could haul back to Nipawin.

In mid January another team arrived. Three men from Lake Lenore, Saskatchewan informed us they had come to do commercial fishing.

I looked over their outfit—one net about eight meshes deep, capable of catching only fifteen to twenty fish at one setting. They asked me where they could fish. "Anywhere on the lake," I said.

I watched these three fellows trying to set their net, and I could see that they had never done it before. The way things were going, it would probably take them a couple of days to complete the job. After two hours they had only begun, because they were attempting to cut holes in three feet of ice and with a pole-axe, the only cutting tool they had. They had not known that, in the winter fishing business, two essentials are the ice chisel and the jigger, an instrument that threads the net under the ice and is moved as the fisherman jerks on an attached line that levers the jigger forward under the ice.

The men's parkas were ice-covered, as they splashed up water while they were chopping at the hole. They had an eighteen-foot pole with a running line tied to one end. This was how they hoped to thread the net along, while they cut another hole every eighteen feet.

I talked to them when I could no longer stand to see what they were doing. I offered to lend them an ice chisel, four standard nets, and the use of a jigger, and I would help them get started in the morning. For these courtesies, they would haul up a load of dry wood from a nearby island both for our camp and for their tent, which they had set up beside our cabin.

They were more than willing and hauled up a second load for me before they left. At the end of the week, they pulled out for home with a half a ton of fish. They told me that they had never fished with a net before in all their lives. This episode is but one example of ill-advised and ill-equipped ventures taken on by inexperienced men in those days when cash was hard to get.

The result of our own winter fishing venture was a no-profit situation. I had hired the men on the basis that we share the proceeds after paying the expenses. Sale of the fish paid for all food, clothing, and equipment. However, there was a small balance owed to our freighter that I would have to pay.

7

FUR TRADER

I N THAT SPRING OF 1931 I decided I was not returning to my
homestead at Torch River Settlement for the summer for it seemed
highly unlikely that I could make any kind of money there even
if I landed some seasonal work. With three of my helpers during
the preceding winter's commercial fishing, namely Tom McDougall, Bob
Fred, and Fred Heinrichs, we struck out northward on the ice for Pelican
Narrows, and our final destination of Flin Flon, in Manitoba. We hoped
to get work in the big mine or the smelter that had been operating there
for a few years before our arrival.

We took our leave of Deschambault Lake on March 28 with some furs
that I had traded with the locals for extra groceries from our fishing supplies. We had made the trade while we were building a fishing cabin on
Spruce Island for future use. In later years this same cabin would serve
as a trading post for the Saskatchewan Government.

Our party reached Pelican Narrows after one day of travel. One of the
locals had a bag of furs that he wanted to freight out to Flin Flon with
his dog team. We made a deal whereby he would haul our packs and we
would supply the groceries for the trip.

Arthur Jan, a free trader at Pelican Narrows, had invited us to stay at
his bunkhouse any time we were travelling that way. Unfortunately both
he and Mrs. Jan had left for Flin Flon shortly before our arrival. Jan
however had arranged with the manager of Revillon Frères Trading Post

to put us up in the company bunkhouse, so we enjoyed a warm comfortable night. In later years, Jan Lake was named in honour of Mr. Jan.

On our way to Flin Flon, we spent the next night at Birch Portage, a tiny Cree village near Birch Rapids on the Sturgeon-weir River. We put up for the night at the home of Andrew Custer, where we spent a pleasant evening and had a good rest. Andrew's son Walter was the only one in the family who could speak English, and he interpreted our conversation with the family into the Cree language and back to English for us. Walter's Cree name was "Strong Man." We saw a photograph of him carrying seven hundred pounds of flour on his way across a portage.

Next evening, after we had arrived in Flin Flon and were looking around for a room, I met Jim Fairburn, an old friend I had not seen since we were game wardens together in 1922 and 1923. Fairburn was an old timer in the North by 1931, having been a trapper and prospector since 1914, and in the Flin Flon area when the first great mineral discovery was made. During the summer months he lived in Prince Albert. We were fortunate to meet him because after our mutual surprise at our meeting he took us to a Greek restaurant, where we found a good place to stay.

After a good wash and general clean-up, we went downstairs to eat. It was 9 P.M., and this was our first meal since noon. Our appetites were understandably robust, but we had only six dollars between us. However, we were running up a bill, so ready cash was not required. The reviving effects of that hearty meal were amazing; as we walked out, we felt fit enough to start on another one hundred mile hike!

Fairburn asked me if I had any furs to sell. On learning that I had pelts, he took me to see Mr. Quincey, a fur buyer and also the proprietor of one of the local pool rooms. I sold the furs for $50, and we split the proceeds among the four of us.

The next morning was April 1, but it was so cold the makeshift wooden plank sidewalks of Flin Flon were held fast in the ankle-deep mud, which had been frozen solid since the first melt of the spring season.

I made enquiries as to the possibility of employment at the mine, but was informed that the mine was laying off workers as an economy measure. Fairburn and I walked over to ask Quincey about any kind of employment. Fairburn himself was getting ready to go spring trapping with a Dutch man I had met in Big River in the early 1920s.

After I had a long conversation with Quincey, he said he would introduce me to a young man named Liard Oulette. He had a good dog team—four strong dogs, said Quincey. He had no money but was a good pool player who managed to make enough money from the employed miners so he did not starve to death. Oulette also spoke Cree. He had, according to Quincey, mentioned that he would like to freight for any trader who might be going into the wilderness to trade for furs.

I let Quincey know I would be interested in such a venture. I would go back to Birch Portage where I had stayed overnight and where I knew several native families who were trapping muskrats and beavers.

Soon afterwards, Oulette showed up in the pool room. Quincey made the introductions and we began to talk. When I proposed the freight haul, Oulette said without any hesitation, "I'm game to go."

I explained that it was some forty miles to Birch Portage. Since we had met a swing of horse teams on their last freighting trip of the season with supplies for Pelican Narrows, we would probably meet them coming back, and thus the road would be open.

"I should be able to make it to Birch Portage in half a day," said Oulette. "I'm used to running behind the toboggan."

When I went on to explain that at this season there could be from five to eight inches of water in places under the new snowfall lying on the lake ice, Oulette reconsidered his travelling time. He now estimated it at one full day to Birch Portage.

In the afternoon of April 2, Quincey and I went over to William Hicks' grocery store, where Quincey bought two hundred pounds of groceries and other trading supplies, including silk scarves, handkerchiefs, and beads.

Early in the morning of April 3, Oulette arrived with his four dogs and sleigh. The sleigh was shod with steel runners, appropriate equipment for spring travel. It was 2 P.M. before we got going. In the first mile we upset the load twice, so that we were forced to affix a pole across the sleigh, tying it firmly on both sides. Then we walked knee deep in snow and water, one on each side, to hold the sleigh from tipping over—a most difficult and awkward mode of travel, yet the only way to make any progress.

It took us until 11 P.M. to get to Allan McDonald's trapping cabin on Annabel Lake, only eleven miles from Flin Flon, and we were very happy to see the light in the cabin window as we pulled in. Here we caught up with Jim Fairburn and his partner on their way to Wildnest Lake. They had three dogs and a sleigh and were finding the travelling to be as difficult as we were. In fact, Fairburn and his partner had found the going so difficult they had divided their load and were hauling half loads in relays.

On the trail next morning, as we travelled on the portage between Annabel and Johnson Lakes, we met the swing of teams of horses and their drivers returning empty from Pelican Narrows. As we were having dinner with the freighters, they warned us of rough going to Birch Portage. The return of cold weather had laid a sheet of thin ice above the slush upon the winter ice. This had caused the horses to break through to the solid lake ice at each step, and the poor beasts were bleeding from cuts on their legs just above the hooves. This thin ice had all been broken down along the trail, and our outfit would be trailing along in water and slush.

We had four miles to travel on Johnson Lake. Through slush and broken ice, it was one of the hardest trips I ever made in the North. We were pulling on the sleigh to help the dogs along.

When the time came for a rest stop, I would tease Oulette about the slow travelling and asked if he still thought we could make it to Birch Portage from Flin Flon in half a day. He replied by asking how far we still had to go.

When we arrived at Granite Lake, it was only four and one-half miles to Birch Portage. After we crossed to the west side, Oulette told me that he had had enough and wanted to make camp. We were resting there for a short time when from a distance we could hear someone chopping wood. Then we laboured on, although we were both dog tired and the dogs themselves all but exhausted. Arriving at the Sturgeon-weir River, we found the going worse than on the lakes, for there was now more water than ever on the ice. I was wading in knee-deep slush while labouring with the sleigh.

Finally two Indians came along: a couple of youths who took our packs and sleeping bags to Andrew Custer's place. Then they returned and helped with the sleigh.

The people at Custer's were very happy to see us and, after an all-around handshaking, they bade us to be seated for they realized we were dead tired. They also recognized me as one of the party who had stopped there recently on our way to Flin Flon and were delighted at the supplies we had brought in.

Our stay at Birch Portage lasted for two days. During this time, we traded our entire load, so that at the final settlement with Quincey we made about $40 for our hard work. The weather had remained very cold, which would likely extend the trapping season. I asked Oulette if he was interested in continuing to haul in supplies and trading until the end of May.

He replied, "Olaf, right now I am only interested in my girl friend in Flin Flon."

So that was that. I would have to look elsewhere for assistance. When we had left Flin Flon, Quincey had told us that if we traded the first load and got back in time to take in another with a horse team, he would finance the venture, providing that there were indications of a good muskrat catch.

I now asked the Indians if they would trade me their furs if I returned with another load of supplies. They readily agreed. I then sent Oulette back to Flin Flon in the company of Johnny Custer, who would freight in the supplies with the horses. They made it to Flin Flon in one day, for they had no load and out on the lakes the road bed had frozen solid.

Walter Custer took me to the cabin of a man who had moved in with relatives. Now I was better set up to do business, in a private cabin furnished with a stove, bunk, bench and small table.

On the third day after Oulette and Walter Custer had left, I began to look for Walter and the horse team, but no one came. On the fourth day I looked in vain again. However, on the fifth day, my supplies arrived with, much to my surprise, my former partner Fred Heinrichs and Oulette as the teamsters. They had made it from Flin Flon to Birch Portage in one and one half days with a large load, assisted by solid ice on the lakes.

Heinrichs gave me some good news. Our partner Tom McDougall had landed a job in The Pas helping Oulette's father with a draying business. Bob Fred had been hired to work under Bill Cox, a boxer and the hall manager at the Community Hall in Flin Flon, where they held dances and various sporting events.

Oulette and Heinrichs left again next morning with a bale of muskrat pelts I had traded. Heinrichs then set out for his home in Nipawin, since I had sent Quincey a note to see that Heinrichs was given enough money to get there. I did not see Oulette again until the late 1930s, when I was on the train from Sherritt Gordon Mines to The Pas. Oulette did indeed marry his girlfriend and spent many years working the northern railways as a brakeman. He certainly proved his prowess to me and to the world at large, for he was an excellent dog musher and for several years consistently won the dog derby held at The Pas each winter.

At Birch Portage I ran out of trading goods on May 1, and Roderick Custer agreed to take me to Flin Flon in his canoe. The canoe route led down the Sturgeon-weir River to Beaver Lake, (officially named Amisk Lake on the map, as *amisk* is Cree for beaver). We arrived at Beaver Lake on the same day that we had set out, and crossed the still-frozen lake on the ice. That night we stayed with another native, Dougall McKenzie, who told us the ice was unsafe but the lake would be open in about a week.

We returned to Birch Portage, arriving there about midnight after a hard day at the paddles. At about 11 A.M. the next day, Roderick Custer and I struck out for Flin Flon on foot, following the winter road on land and skirting the lakes en route. We were packing six hundred muskrat pelts along with some other furs plus enough food to last us for two days. We walked until dark that first day and made camp on the portage between Johnson Lake and Annabel Lake. We were now twenty-five miles from Flin Flon.

I noticed that the north side of Annabel Lake was fairly level jack pine country and very good for walking, so that after a good sleep we proceeded on this course, travelling where part of the Hanson Lake Road runs today, but in that spring of 1931 there was of course no road at all. Custer and I were trying to make it to Flin Flon by the best possible land route so we were avoiding creeks and muskegs, which at that time of the year were full of water.

We made it to Annabel Creek at about 4 P.M. By the present day highway, it is eight miles from this point to Creighton, but at that particular time I estimate our trail ran for twenty miles on the devious route we were forced to take around various lakes and bays.

Every time we climbed to the top of a hill, Roderick would exclaim, "I see the big stove pipe!"

This was the Indian name for the gigantic smelter stack, which is visible for miles from any high hill in the entire region. Sometimes we had to walk away from the stack to get around open water. With three hundred muskrat pelts on my back, it seemed to me that we would never get to Flin Flon.

When the sun had gone down, we began to hear noises of people working around the mine site. Then we arrived at Flin Flon Lake and walked across the dam in the dark. There were several railroad tracks leading away from the area, but fortunately we took the one which led us into town.

We walked into Quincey's place at about 11 P.M. They were still up and quite surprised to see us come in at that hour. Quincey was also pleased with the quality and quantity of the pelts we had brought. When he learned that I had another five hundred and sixty pelts cached at Birch Portage, he asked how I was planning to bring them in and take out more supplies.

"I want to rent a canoe," I told him.

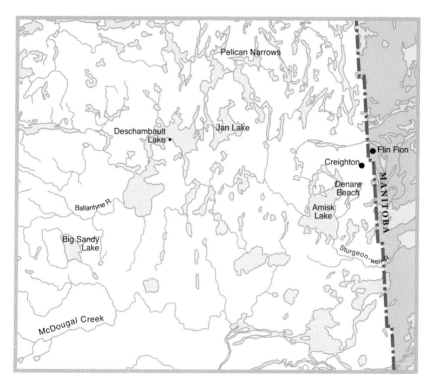

During the 1930s Hanson trapped and traded fur in the Jan Lake area as far north as Pelican Narrows and as far east as Flin Flon.

"I suggest you buy one at Keddy Hardware," he said. "There's a good one for sale there."

By this time, Mrs. Quincey had prepared a very good midnight dinner, after which Custer left to stay with friends in town, promising to rejoin me in the morning.

I was at Keddy's when they opened in the morning, and I bought the canoe, a sixteen-foot Chestnut, well built, with cedar planking and ribs, and an outer covering of canvas with a slick hard finish. I paid $115 after haggling until I got two paddles included in the original price.

Next, I bought five hundred pounds of supplies and dry goods at Bill Hughes' grocery store and had the goods packed and ready to leave for Beaver Lake next morning. I had hired a teamster to haul our outfit with his team and wagon from Flin Flon to Phantom Lake, and we would canoe and pack over the portages for the rest of the way.

The water route at this end was new to me, but Roderick Custer was well acquainted with it. He informed me that there were fourteen portages from Phantom Lake to Beaver Lake. He was a good strong packer and carried from two hundred and fifty to three hundred pounds on the portages, using a tumpline. I used a packsack and carried the canoe while Roderick was taking a turn at packing freight.

This was my first introduction to canoe travel as it had been in the north for centuries. I found it to be a pleasure, and I did not mind the packing on the portages. On the first portage I packed the canoe across, a distance of about a mile. Then I portaged our food supplies while Roderick took over the trading goods in two trips. Until now I had travelled overland and across lakes on the winter ice. When I was a game guardian, I had travelled by canoe, but I had always hired a native to take me where I was going.

The next thirteen portages were short ones, as we followed Meridian Creek down to Beaver Lake. We crossed Mystic Lake, two small lakes, then Table Lake, and reached Beaver Lake after dark.

Next morning we pulled the canoe over drift ice on the lake, one man on each side of the canoe to balance it on its keel so that the canvas would not be damaged. The ice had blocked our passage to the open lake. After we reached open water, we traversed ten miles of open lake to the south shore at a place called Beaver City. What had seemed a populous place turned out to be nothing more than a few dilapidated cabins occupied by a lone native trapper named Angus McDonald. After a short rest, we paddled on to Dougall McKenzie's place, where we slept. The next day we paddled and poled upriver to Birch Portage.

Roderick had meanwhile introduced me to the tumpline—I had had no previous experience with this device. After my first try I had to give it up, for use of the line puts great strain on the neck muscles, in my case causing severe soreness. A good tumpline is made of strong, good quality leather. The centre of the strap is about three inches wide and rests across the forehead while the two joining straps are narrower and are usually attached to a wooden grub box, one strap on each side. On this box the packer can load as much freight as he wishes to carry. The weight lies against his back while both hands are free, but the packer frequently holds onto the straps at a height above the shoulders as he walks with the load. Indians who regularly pack in this manner load up to seven hundred pounds and develop strong oversized neck muscles. The novice must train himself gradually, increasing his load as his neck strengthens.

In the spring of 1931, the month of May remained unusually cold. The trapping season closed officially on May 15, but trapping continued unofficially that year for fur such as muskrat, and beaver pelt remained prime as long as the water was still cold. That year trappers plied their lines until June 1.

I planned to also leave Birch Portage by that date as my trading venture would be wound up for the season. All the native families except a very few were back from their trapping grounds. Those who had returned were busy planting small vegetable gardens. On the last day of May, the last family arrived, with thirty raw, unstretched muskrat pelts and nine beaver pelts.

At that time beaver trapping was tightly controlled because the animals were scarce, so only a few beaver were allotted per family. They could be sold legally only to Dominion Fur Sales in Winnipeg and only by the Government of Saskatchewan. This family could sell only six beaver pelts legally. I already had four illegal pelts, so why not take three more? A police constable at Pelican Narrows was administering the beaver program in his area and keeping a watchful eye out, but it would be the same fine if I were caught with a sheep instead of a lamb.

The next day I left Birch Portage. Three packers carried my load across the portage of the same name. They loaded my canoe, eyed it briefly, and declared I could run the rapids all the way to Beaver Lake on my return trip to Flin Flon.

The first of the rapids was called Leaf Rapids and was by far the roughest of the trip, and the first that I had ever run alone. As I entered the first chute, the canoe's keel struck a huge boulder, causing the canoe to rock violently. I ran on down the rapid after shipping about two pails of water. Below the rapid, I dragged the canoe to shore, where I unloaded everything and dumped out the water, at the same time considering myself very lucky for a greenhorn.

The next portage was at Scoop Rapids, so named because a traveller could scoop out fish with a hand net at its downstream end. Fish could not swim upstream at this spot because there is a waterfall below, in which one could see dozens of fish milling about, trying to ascend the falls. The Indians always kept a net with a long pole handle there, so that most times in the spring and again in the fall a traveller could scoop out whitefish, pickerel, and jackfish. Only in the months of July and August might one have difficulty in finding fish at this spot.

I have enjoyed several meals of fish there as I travelled the river in the years that followed. There was even a very nice camping place below the rapid where you could enjoy a scenic view while eating your fish. I always made it a point to stop there any time I travelled on that section of the Sturgeon-weir River.

I did not take the risk of running Snake Rapids, the next obstacle. This rapid is about a mile long. Roderick Custer had cautioned me that I should let the canoe down on a rope while I walked on the shore. I was a long time descending that rapid, but when I had passed through my furs were dry and safe. Finally I packed everything across Spruce Portage, the last on the river. Then I stopped to make my supper. Now I paddled down to Dougall McKenzie's cabin at the mouth of the Sturgeon-weir River on Beaver Lake, arriving there at about 8 P.M.

Since it was a nice calm evening, I began to paddle straight for Beaver City and Angus McDonald's trapping cabin one mile north of the Sturgeon-weir outlet. After I had gone six or seven miles across the lake, a breeze began to blow from the south-east so that I was now paddling against the wind. It was getting dusk, but I could still see Big Island lying just off the point of land near my destination. The head wind strengthened and the sky began to cloud over. The point of land was drawing closer, but the waves became larger as the wind velocity increased. I paddled on until I got in the lee of the point, where the waves subsided somewhat.

I was certain that I could now paddle safely to my destination. As I rounded the point for the two-mile paddle to Angus McDonald's cabin, the waves were running high against me. I kept close to shore, but the wind grew stronger. My progress grew very slow indeed, little more than a crawl. The wind, erratic for the past short while, now suddenly calmed.

I plied my paddle with increased vigour because the sky had completely clouded over. It was very dark.

Suddenly I could see McDonald's dock dead ahead. All his dogs began to bark and howl, and a light came on in the cabin. He called off the dogs while I beached the canoe and tied it fast. I walked up to the cabin, identified myself, and asked if I could stay there for the night. He came out and helped me carry my fur bales to the cabin, and we placed my equipment in a shed near the dock.

It was 1 A.M. I had been paddling and portaging since 8 A.M. and had covered forty-seven miles. McDonald remembered me from the time I had stopped there earlier and now hastened to make a pot of tea to go with the food that I had with me. While we were eating, the wind changed to the northwest, and by the time we turned in, the lake was a mass of boiling white caps as the fury of the wind bore down on this ten-mile stretch of open water. I was grateful for a safe dry bunk.

When we arose next morning, I told McDonald that I had thirty raw muskrat pelts to stretch and dry. He brought me a good supply of stretchers to do the job. After a late breakfast, I opened my bales of fur and found that three of the beaver pelts had gotten slightly wet when I had run down Leaf Rapids the day before. I spread these behind the stove to dry.

Outside there was a cold wind blowing down the lake; white caps were everywhere and there was rain. It was not a day for canoe travel on Beaver Lake. No matter, I could pass the time stretching and drying my muskrat skins.

I had completed about ten pelts before we had lunch. Back at my work afterwards, I had almost finished when we heard the dogs begin to bark furiously. When we looked out, we saw two figures out in the heavy rain, pulling a canoe up on the beach. Needless to say, we were very surprised at this development, for it was most unlikely to see canoe travellers out in such miserable weather. From where we stood our visitors appeared to be a man and a woman, which caused McDonald to observe, "Must be some trapper and his wife."

"I had better hide the beaver pelts," I said. I had three lying behind the stove and four more hanging on the wall when McDonald went out to talk to the visitors. As he left, he assured me that only trappers stopped at his place, and these probably had more beaver pelts to sell.

When McDonald had left, I decided to hide the beaver pelts anyway. The only place that looked good for this purpose was under his bunk.

I lifted the mattress and tucked them underneath. Then I returned to my work at the pelts. Just then, the outside door opened. As I looked up, I saw a man in the uniform of the Royal Canadian Mounted Police!

"Hello," I recall saying to the newcomer.

I think he answered the same way. He told me he was almost frozen from battling the wind, waves, rain, and cold. Large snowflakes mixed with driving rain had pelted him and his assistant as they paddled for this landing when their outboard motor had broken down.

I was busy thinking that I was in about as awkward a position with the law as I had ever been before. Here I was, caught red-handed with thirty fresh muskrat pelts, obviously trapped during the closed season. While McDonald helped the Mountie's assistant stow away their outfit in the shed by the dock, the Mountie himself looked at the bags of muskrat pelts and the fresh skins hanging from the rafters above his head.

He asked if I was the trader from Birch Portage. I replied that I was that person, and we introduced ourselves.

"It looks bad for me to have fresh skins in my possession at this time of year," I began lamely.

"Well," answered the Mountie slowly. "Are these pelts all fresh, or did some just get wet on your travels and you are re-drying them?"

"Some got wet at Leaf Rapids, but some are fresh," I confessed.

The Mountie was warming himself by the stove.

"Let us say that you are only re-drying the lot you have here," he said.

"Thank you," was all I could say, as I felt very much relieved.

Then McDonald re-entered the cabin with Arthur Morin, Special Constable and Interpreter from Pelican Narrows.

Now that everything had settled down to normal, I began to worry about the seven hidden beaver pelts. The Mountie was telling us that they had broken the drive shaft in their outboard motor when the propeller had struck a rock in the Sturgeon-weir River. When the wind had changed to the northwest, they had hoisted a sail on their nineteen-foot freighter canoe and finally reached this landing while carrying five bales of beaver pelts destined for Dominion Fur Sales in Winnipeg.

McDonald had a six-horse-power outboard motor. The Mountie then made a deal with him to haul the beaver pelts to Flin Flon.

After a while, Angus McDonald went out to feed his dogs for their evening meal. I went with him so that I could tell him where I had hidden the beaver pelts, but he asked me for that information before I had a chance. When I told him, he decided that they would be all right there until morning.

"Are you going to take the beaver pelts with you to Flin Flon?" he asked. It had been arranged that McDonald would tow my canoe and the Mountie's—in short we were going to be travelling, camping, and portaging together.

"If you have a good hiding place for the beaver pelts, we will cache them there until I can come back and pick them up," I suggested.

"I have a good place," said McDonald. "My stove is sitting on the bottom of a big wooden packing box; the top is open and resting on the floor. We'll hide them under the box."

Early next morning, the wind was down as we were all busy loading the canoes. McDonald had advised me privately to leave my sleeping bag in the cabin until the canoes were loaded. That task completed, McDonald returned to lock the door while I trailed along to fetch my sleeping bag. As soon as we were inside, McDonald grabbed a big butcher knife and jabbed it under the edge of the box, prying up box and stove until he got his fingers under the edge. I, meanwhile, had dug the pelts out from under the mattress and tucked them neatly under the box while McDonald let it down to the floor. It was about as neat a cache as I have ever seen.

As we returned to the dock, the Mountie and Arthur Morin had already launched their canoe. McDonald pushed out his craft and tied the police canoe to the stern of his own. I tied up to the stern of the police canoe.

The weather was clear and sunny, and there was only a light breeze blowing. In forty-five minutes, we had crossed Beaver Lake and entered the mouth of Meridian Creek. However, we still had a big day ahead of us, for we faced the fourteen portages to Phantom Lake. On the portages, I carried one packsack of fur with another packsack piled on top, this one containing my clothes and two bearskins, which I had taken in trade, in a roll.

On the first portage we caught up with Dougall McKenzie and his son, who were taking in their furs to trade in Flin Flon. We were now a travelling party of six men and four canoes. When we had crossed five portages, we called a stop for dinner. We finished off the bacon and eggs the Mountie had brought from Pelican Narrows plus pork and beans and bannock from my supplies. By 7:30 P.M., we had reached the long portage into Phantom Lake. Here we cooked our supper, which was a repetition of dinner—minus the eggs.

The Mountie wanted to get to Flin Flon that night, which meant we had to get back to work at once, packing over the portage. It was black night before everything had been moved across. The policeman asked to use one of my packsacks. I handed it over, whereupon he put it on his back, placed one bag of beaver pelts across it, then another bag lengthwise across the load so he could steady it by holding on with one hand as he walked. He turned out to be an excellent packer, and I was surprised to see the way he was working. On this final portage, there was a short stretch of muskeg, where we walked on poles to avoid sinking to our knees in the bog. The Mountie was walking ahead of me, and he slipped off into the water as he began to cross on the poles. Then he began to take the bags one by one over this treacherous place. When I caught up to him. I helped him move some of his load across the mire.

As I was helping him to re-load, placing the bag of beaver skins over my packsack once more strapped to his back, I could hear the crackling of my dry bearskins, the same sound that comes from dry beaver pelts when you squeeze them together. I began to think about this, and I contemplated the possibility that he might open my packsack to investigate the suspicious sound that was not unlike that of beaver pelts.

I found out the next day that the Mountie never did look into that packsack. McDonald told me that the policeman had voiced his suspicions and asked if I had beaver pelts in that particular packsack. McDonald had assured him that I had two bearskins only, and the man of the law let it go at that. I believe the man was concerned that, if he had unwittingly carried illicit furs across the portage on my behalf and the story became known in Flin Flon, he would have to take the merciless ribbing from some of the inhabitants as well as from his fellow police officers.

Our Mountie had proved himself to be a very fine gentleman with sound judgement, and I found this to be the case with most police officers I met in the North. They were doing good work, helping the natives and whites alike. Their role in crime prevention would be difficult to record in full. They were highly respected for the struggles and hardships they had to face in those days and always helped me when I needed it.

We beached our canoes at the north end of Phantom Lake at about 11 P.M. I unloaded, draped my tarpaulin over the fur packs, and tipped the canoe over my cargo in case it should rain.

The Mountie made ready to hike the remaining few miles to Flin Flon. He instructed Morin to stay right there and camp, while keeping an eye on the beaver pelts. As he began to pack some of his effects into a suitcase and made ready to leave, I offered to accompany him into town and carry some of his bags. He accepted with delight and offered to pay me, which I flatly refused.

We were in Flin Flon by midnight. The Greek café was still open. The Mountie took a room, where we went to wash up. Then he treated me to a steak and apple pie. He wanted me to take a room, but I was concerned about my fur packs at Phantom Lake.

When I returned there at about 1:30 A.M., everyone was asleep out in the open. I unrolled my sleeping bag on a level place and turned in. It was a beautiful clear night and too cold for mosquitoes. I was looking up at the stars and listening to the noise of the big mine when I dropped off to sleep.

When I awoke, the sun was up and Dougall McKenzie and his son were making tea over the campfire. Angus McDonald was complaining about the poor sleep he had had that night—he could not get comfortable. We all had a good laugh when we saw that he had been sleeping on some broken rocks. Morin and I were the last to rise, and we did so without any complaints.

In about an hour, a teamster drove up with his horses and wagon. The Mountie had sent him out to pick up his fur bales and our freight. As I would soon be coming back this way to retrieve my beaver pelts at McDonald's, I hoisted my canoe on my shoulders planning to cache it in a safe place away from the main trail. As I was leaving the main landing area, hurrying to avoid delaying our party, I came upon some loose boards scattered about. I did not see the rusty four-inch spike protruding from one of the boards. It plunged through the sole of my ankle rubber, moccasin, and sock, completely through my foot and up through the top of my rubber boot.

I dropped the canoe. I had to put my other foot on the board to pull my foot off the spike. Then I carried the canoe to its hiding-place.

I walked only about halfway to town when I could no longer follow the team and wagon. It had been better to walk that far, for the terrain there was very rocky. My foot felt as though I was walking on a football. When we finally arrived in Flin Flon, I hobbled painfully right over to Quincey's and said, "Get me to a doctor fast."

By this time my foot had swelled to the ankle. I could no longer force it into my rubber, so I was only wearing a sock.

The doctor said it was a bad wound. He tried unsuccessfully to drain some blood from it. Then he bandaged and taped up my foot. In those times, antibiotics had not yet come to Flin Flon. I managed to hop along to the café, carrying one rubber in my hand. I had supper and soon after crawled into my bed.

I did not sleep at all that night, however, for there was steady throbbing pain. I had to loosen the bandages for my foot was still swelling. When I examined my foot in the night, it had indeed swollen, until it looked like a football with five toes sticking out of one end.

In the morning I tried to go downstairs for breakfast, but I found that I could not put any weight on that foot at all; the pain was just too great. I did get to the washroom and managed to get back into bed.

There was another guest in the adjoining room, and he saw me hopping to the washroom. He came in and asked, "Did you get hurt while working at the mine?"

"No," I answered, "yesterday I stepped on a four inch spike, and now I am suffering for it."

After I told him the facts, he asked, "Is there anything I can do for you?"

"Go downstairs and get me a cup of coffee and a sandwich and charge it to my account, if you will be so kind."

He did me this favour and left. I never saw him again. When I settled my bill a few days later, I found that the coffee and sandwich were not included; apparently the stranger had paid for them. The amount, thirty cents, looked good in 1931.

The doctor had asked me to return if the swelling in my foot had not subsided somewhat by morning. Now I was thinking of doing just that. Then Jim Fairburn walked into the room, having just learned from Quincey that I had put a spike through my foot. I was certainly glad to see him again. We visited for a while, talking about my trading experiences and his trapping activities since we had last met.

Then he asked me to let him have a look at my throbbing foot.

"Looks real bad," he muttered. "Too bad I wasn't around when this happened, for then I would have had you walking around today. Don't put the bandage back on. I'm leaving right now and will be back in a few minutes to doctor this foot."

He returned shortly with a small bottle of turpentine and some clean cloths. First, he tipped the bottle over the hole where the spike had entered my foot. Next, he tipped the mouth of the bottle over the hole where the spike had protruded. He went through this performance twice. Then he padded the wound on top and bottom of the foot with turpentine-soaked cloths and bandaged everything snug with the original bandage.

"You'll be able to walk down the steps for supper by 6 P.M.," he said.

The turpentine took hold with a terrific burning pain, which lasted for about fifteen minutes. My foot seemed to be on fire. Quickly the pain eased off, and the foot felt much better. Fairburn brought up my dinner, so that I did not have to use the stairs. He left me then, promising to be back by 6 P.M.

Fairburn did return after he had spent the afternoon playing several games of pool. A good player, he had cashed in several times while playing pea pool, whereupon the game had broken up when the other players had all hung up their cues. Fairburn had outclassed his opponents.

Much to my amazement, I walked down the stairs that evening. The swelling in my foot had begun to subside.

"Tomorrow you'll be wearing both your rubbers," said Fairburn.

It was hard to believe, but I did just that. That next day, my foot began to bleed and I changed the dressing three times. I could however put my full weight on that foot with little pain. The healing process was almost complete after a few more days.

Fairburn accompanied me on my return trip to Angus McDonald's place to pick up my hidden beaver pelts. Fairburn had also supplied two mosquito bars so we could sleep at night. The weather had at last warmed up, and the mosquitoes were hatching in their millions. We walked through clouds of them on every portage and suffered from their stings, since repellents as we know them now did not exist at that time. At night, safe under our mosquito bars, we listened to their blood-song.

Fairburn was a prospector at heart, and we spent one afternoon looking over some rock formations. He said that Beaver Lake had good indications for gold and copper. Though we spent a very interesting half day there, we found neither gold nor copper on that trip.

On the way back to Flin Flon, Fairburn packed our entire load of one hundred and twenty-five pounds, using a tumpline. I had no trouble packing the canoe by favouring my healing foot.

When I had brought in the last of the muskrats and my accounts were tallied, I discovered that I was nine dollars in debt. Then I found a furlegger who bought my beaver pelts, so I finished my trading venture twenty-one dollars ahead after I had paid for my canoe and all expenses.

I was not exactly prospering. Considering all my hard work and the hardships and risk involved, this venture had been a failure financially. As for experience and knowledge gained, my account had received a great boost.

8

STRUGGLE FOR SURVIVAL
IN FLIN FLON

EVERY MORNING I WENT to the mine, looking for work. Miners and helpers were being paid about forty cents an hour, and any vacancies were much sought after. There was always a line-up waiting for someone to be injured or killed, when someone new would be hired. After a while I gave up trying. The Great Depression was at its height.

Fairburn was in the same boat that I was. We camped together on Ross Lake Island near Flin Flon, where there was one grocery store and a few log shacks. We pitched our tent in the woods just north of the store, where we sat one day contemplating what we might do to eke out a living for the next few months until the trapping season opened once again.

Fairburn now turned to his ability as a man with a pool cue. He came up with a plan whereby we could both make a few dollars. The habitués of the three pool halls in town were onto him, and when he too often cashed in at the popular game of pea pool, they would quit the game and try to reorganize another session at one of the other two establishments.

Hanson giving one of his colleagues
an outdoor haircut.

In the game, a number of participants received a numbered pea from a leather bottle. If a player could sink or pocket the ball with his number, he collected the stake (set at twenty-five cents or more) from each of the other players. If before that he had sunk any ball corresponding to another player's pea, that player paid him an additional stake or ante.

Fairburn's plan was to out-smart the pea-pool gamblers. I as his helper would only play pool with the non-gamblers as a pastime. We would separate, and I would act as undercover man by locating the pea pool game as soon as it was going, then I would locate Fairburn, who was always playing snooker somewhere in another hall. I would signal him by placing one, two, or three fingers on my hat brim to tell him where the pea pool game was going. This gave Fairburn a chance to hot-foot it over there and play at least one game before it broke up because he had made some tremendous shot, sunk his own ball and cashed in. No one seemed to catch on to how he got to the game so quickly, for sometimes the game had not yet started when he arrived there. One man once protested that Fairburn was a professional. His game mates disagreed, saying that they all knew him as a trapper and prospector of long standing. We made enough from his winnings to keep us in groceries for some time.

In that summer of 1931, there was a good crop of wild strawberries. I picked and sold strawberries for a week, averaging about ten pounds a day, which I sold for a dollar and fifty cents each day, or fifteen cents a pound. I had to walk about ten miles from town towards Beaver Lake, where an area of the countryside had been burned off in 1928. The best berries grew there, but I never saw anyone else picking berries while I was working at it. Then heavy rain fell for three days, which put an end to my strawberry business.

We had to make other plans if we were to continue to eat. Fairburn and I had a little talk with Quincey, who had financed my trading venture. I informed him that I had a commercial fishing outfit and a camp at Deschambault Lake. I would need twenty more nets for next winter's fishing. We also needed to build another camp on Jan Lake, where the Indians had told me there were numerous trout and very large whitefish. Quincey was interested in this proposition at once. He agreed to advance us one hundred dollars and supplies to last us for one month, so that we could go to Jan Lake and build the camp as soon as possible.

In late July, we set out paddling across Beaver Lake in calm weather. As we neared the west shore, we rounded an island where on the shore we saw a very nice camping place with some tent poles leaning against a spruce tree. It was only 7 P.M. so the sun was still above the horizon, but the campsite looked so inviting we laid up for the night. Besides, islands are sometimes less infested with mosquitoes than is the mainland.

We pitched the tent and spent the evening reading stories from magazines we had brought in case we became storm bound while on our travels. We also had a deck of cards and a cribbage board. As we were about to turn in for the night, we saw a great heavy black storm cloud moving closer from the west. We carried the canoe off the beach to the edge of the woods and turned it upside down over our groceries and equipment. As it was still very calm, we neglected to secure our tent more than is usually required.

At about 3 A.M. we awoke to a tremendous thunderclap. The lightning struck so close that we were dazed for a few moments. When a few drops of rain struck the tent and more thunder and lightening followed in the distance, we heard a mounting roar. I got up and had only partly dressed when the wind hit the tent. It took the two of us to hold the tent from being blown off the island. There was a deluge of rain descending. When the wind eased off, more soaking rain fell while we sat on our bedrolls and held up the tent with our heads to keep the bedding dry. It had rained for about an hour when dawn began to break. Then it eased off.

I went to check the groceries, which were in good order, for everything had been securely covered with a tarp. The canoe had been blown away. I found it top side up, caught in some trees and containing several pails of water. But for the trees, it would surely have been blown out into the lake, leaving us stranded. After that experience, I always tied my canoe so that it would not get blown away at night, a precaution I recommend for any wilderness canoe traveller.

We lost half a day drying out our bedding and clothes. Then the route led up the Sturgeon-weir River and to Pelican Narrows, where we arrived five days after leaving Flin Flon.

One day later, at Deschambault Lake, I looked up some of the natives—I knew them all. These people had become interested in prospecting. They sat around the campfire and told us many tales of the gold and silver they had found. One chap said he had found very nice silver as bright as a two-bit piece or maybe brighter. We made an agreement with him that if he could guide us to this place, we would supply the groceries and give him a half interest in the mine, if indeed there should ever be one there.

We left our canoe and outfit with this man's wife, and with the three of us paddling we set out for the silver strike. After crossing five portages, we arrived at the site by 5 P.M.

Jim Fairburn looked closely at the shiny material in the outcropping of the rock and said with some disgust, "I expected this. It's white iron pyrite. or fool's gold. A fresh break is very white for a few days, but oxidation turns it bronzy. It's worthless."

Our guide looked crestfallen. I don't think he believed us at first. We had lost two days just to come here and assess this find—nothing but a wild goose chase. The next day, we paddled wearily back.

Proceeding to my fishing camp at Deschambault Lake, we picked up two axes and a large rip saw. I had taken this saw in trade for groceries in the previous winter. It was so large that at the time I did not think I would ever use it.

The Indians had given us directions on how to get to Jan Lake, and we soon departed. After we had found the portage and crossed over to Pelican Lake, we made our overnight camp on the first island. The next morning, we followed the east shoreline of Pelican Lake until we passed through the narrows into Jan Lake.

It was a pleasant surprise when Fairburn and I first saw Jan Lake. To begin with, it was a fine calm sunny day. Bright clear water and sunny woods were everywhere, giving the impression of a quiet land, uninhabited and clean, far from the worries of the outside world.

We stopped on a peninsula, where we made a pot of tea to go with our bacon and bannock. Looking eastward, where there were several islands lying on the horizon, we thought one island appeared particularly attractive, for it had a long sandy beach. After lunch we paddled directly to this island. It had a beach indeed, one of the finest I have ever seen up this way. After landing and looking about, we decided we had found the beauty spot of the North. The south end of the island was an ideal place to build a camp. It had only a few scattered large spruce trees near the beach but a heavy thick stand of timber to the north to give us shelter. Off shore to the southward, there were two other islands fairly close by.

The tent was set up, a short piece of fishnet set out, and we had fish in our frying pan in short order. Then we began to cut logs for our cabin.

This structure was to be eighteen feet wide and twenty-four feet long. To hurry things along, we made a trip to Deschambault Lake, where we hired two Indians to help us with the logs. We completed building the cabin of peeled logs, gathered a large quantity of sphagnum moss, and piled it nearby to use in chinking the log structure later on.

If anyone had told me I would live there for the next five years, I would have believed him. If anyone had told me I could live here for the rest of my life, I would have answered that I would be happy to do so. As it turned out, I did spend part of my life there—happy and worry-free years—and I look back on this spot with fond memories.

On our return to Flin Flon on August 19 because our groceries and cash had run out, Fairburn and I set up our tent on Ross Lake Island. I killed time in town by playing pool or just talking to the fellows in the pool room. Fairburn again pursued the game of pea pool to raise grocery money.

One day I went back to where I had picked strawberries earlier in the season. To my astonishment I found that blueberries were ripe and growing profusely all over the hills. I had a good feed, but since I had brought no container, I picked my hat full and went home. Fairburn was having supper when I arrived, so we had blueberries for dessert.

That evening I went down to the pool hall to see if anyone wanted to buy blueberries. I soon had orders for one hundred pounds. For the next two weeks, I kept myself busy picking and selling blueberries. On my best day I harvested sixty pounds and did quite well selling them at ten cents a pound.

One day in the pool room, Quincey told me there was a gentleman named Webster staying at the New Richmond Hotel. This man was from Regina, and he was looking for a man with a canoe for one or two days of work at Phantom Lake. I lost no time in contacting this prospective employer. He turned out to be an Inspector of Mining Claims for the Government of Canada. Webster asked me to be at the hotel at 7:30 next morning and to bring a tea pail and two cups, while he provided the food.

When we met in the morning, Webster asked me to wait and he would return shortly. I did not realize that he had gone to hire a teamster with horses and wagon to haul the canoe to Phantom Lake for the price of three dollars. For that money, I could have packed the canoe myself and reached the lake before the team got there.

Webster's work that day was to inspect trenches and assess the work to confirm that the claim holders were complying with their obligations to hold their claims. He had a map showing all claim locations. With this map we had no difficulty at all in finding them all, where we measured the depth, width, and length of each work trench.

Back at the landing after paddling around the lake, it was 6:30 P.M. Webster asked me to walk to town for a team and wagon to haul the canoe back.

"Forget the team," I said. "I can pack the canoe back myself in less time and at the same cost as hired transport."

He looked at me for a moment. Then he asked, "Do you need any help with the canoe?"

"None at all," I replied.

"Very well, Hanson," he said, "meet me at my hotel when you get back to town, and I'll pay you for your work.

With that, he was off on foot. I tied my paddles across the canoe thwarts and padded them with my jacket. Then I shouldered the canoe, hiking along at a trot for the two-mile carry. Before reaching Flin Flon, I had almost caught up to Webster, but he never looked back. I was trying to get to the hotel ahead of him, but I was a few seconds behind, for he was already in his room when I arrived there.

When I knocked on his door, he was quite surprised to see me and asked, "Have you left the canoe on the trail somewhere?"

"No," I answered, "the canoe is at Quincey's place, where we picked it up this morning."

We washed up and went out for a beer together. He paid me nine dollars wages and three dollars for bringing in the canoe, twelve dollars in all, which was four days' wages based on the average rate in 1931.

When the next day I had another good go with the blueberries, I thought that I was doing very well indeed.

Webster and I had talked about the country where I had trapped and fished commercially. I told him of the fishing camp we had built at Jan Lake that summer. Jan Lake was marked on the map in those days, but the full size was not shown and much detail was lacking. We also noted a sizeable body of water between Jan Lake and Beaver Lake, which bore the improbable name of Turd Lake. I had never been there, but I knew that it had once been fished commercially by an outfit named Normans and Enerson. There had been a white trapper there named Jackson, so some people called it Jackson Lake. This lake too was to affect me personally one day.

After the blueberry season had tapered off, I tried to promote the sale of wild cranberries, which were also quite abundant. The venture failed for lack of demand.

At that time there was a freight road being built from Flin Flon to Beaver Lake. The purpose of this road was to haul mining ore from some distant gold mine to the smelter in town. Some wag had spread the rumour that the road was for hauling gold bricks. It was an ambitious project, with much blasting and filling to be done. Fairburn and I went to see if we could get work on the road, but we were told that only dried-out farmers from the south would be hired for this project. We went back to our tent.

"Well, we tried, Jim," I said.

It was time to recruit help for our fishing venture coming up that winter. I went over and talked to Bob "Tiny" Fred, a giant of a man who had worked with us in the previous season. He had grown tired of his job at the Community Hall and said that he would be pleased to return. Fairburn introduced me to Harold Lowder, a fellow pool player, and I asked him to have supper with me at the café. Lowder told me that he was on the waiting list at the mine, but it seemed unlikely that he would be called. He had no fishing experience and no money to buy winter clothes, so I assured him I would teach him how to fish and I would buy him the parka, cap, mitts, moccasins, rubbers, etc. that he would need. He joined our group. The fifth member was John Johnson, a greenhorn who wanted to go fishing and trapping.

After we had made all the arrangements for the supplies we found a man who would freight out our fish for three-and-one-half cents a pound. His name was Bill James, and his price seemed reasonable at the time.

As we had only my small canoe, which was inadequate to transport our sizeable load to Jan Lake, I talked to our freighter, James. As a result of this meeting, he rented us two canoes, a sixteen-foot model similar to mine and a nineteen-foot freighter model. We had twenty-eight hundred pounds of freight, and we would be heavily loaded when our own weight, that of five men, was added to the three canoes.

We left Flin Flon behind on October 12, 1931. Even though we travelled part way by hired transport on the partially completed road to Beaver Lake, it still took us three long hard days to get to Beaver Lake. Most of the time was taken up by portaging our freight.

At Beaver Lake we were greeted by rolling white caps created by a cold high wind. At supper time I assessed the situation and told our crew we had better get Angus McDonald to tow our canoes across the lake. With his outboard motor and some of our freight in his canoe, we would be much better situated for open lake travel. Otherwise we would surely get into trouble in rough water.

That evening three of us put our bedrolls and some groceries into the big canoe and paddled across the lake to Angus McDonald's place. It was a gruelling trip fighting a side wind, and we were soaked with spray as the waves struck the canoe broadside. We were in luck, for Angus was willing to tow us across as soon as the wind let up.

In the morning McDonald towed our canoe back to where Fairburn and Johnson were waiting. The canoes were loaded and ready, tied one behind the other, a brigade of four canoes now being taken across the open lake using McDonald's six-horsepower motor to do the work. The trip back to McDonald's was uneventful because the wind was down.

After we resumed the journey to the mouth of the Sturgeon-weir River, a strong wind began to blow from the west. When the waves began to crest and spray fell on the loaded canoes, McDonald headed for the nearest point of land, for this would have us running with the waves. Half way to the point, I knew the waves were getting higher and we were in trouble. I signalled to McDonald to head for shore as soon as possible. Our big freighter canoe was taking water over the stern, though Fairburn held his sweater over the top to keep out some of the water.

As we were close to shore now, McDonald stopped the motor. Bob and Harold jumped out of the canoe and stood waist deep in the water. The shoreline was all broken limestone, which would have holed the canoes had we tried to land the normal way. Instead the canoes would have to be untied and eased into shore.

Even so, the big canoe struck a rock, which ripped a hole in the canvas covering, and it soon filled with water. John and I managed to save our loads, but all our flour, sugar and oatmeal lay awash in the big canoe. It took all six of us to unload the big freighter. Standing waist deep in the water, we passed the freight from one man to another and finally piled it on shore, one piece at a time.

Now came the chore of drying out the soggy cargo. We hung dry goods over poles to dry in the sun and wind, and we kindled a good fire beside a high limestone cliff. Here the clothing dried out quickly.

With our foodstuffs it was another story. The flour was in twenty-five pound bags, four bags sewn into a burlap cover. We cut open the burlap and spread the bags on the limestone rocks to dry, then spread out the oatmeal and sugar bags in the same manner. The oatmeal turned out to be a total loss, for it formed hard lumps as it dried. Some of the sugar had turned into a white syrup, which leaked from the bags and formed pools on the flat limestone rocks. Some of this liquid was spooned up.

We all slept in the tent that night with an open fire just outside the entrance and the tent flaps tied open to let in some warmth.

In the morning, the white caps were still rolling in the lake, so we spent the day patching two of our canoes and drying our goods. When we set out again for the mouth of the Sturgeon-weir River, the weather had become warm and the wind was calm. The storm had blown itself out.

Our outfit was across Beaver Lake. Another day and Angus McDonald helped us over Spruce Portage and seven miles farther on at Snake Portage. He left us then and headed his canoe for home. We continued on, though it was hard work paddling against the current and sweating on the portages, cold and in danger when we decided to wade our loaded canoes up some lesser rapids while some of the men helped from shore by pulling the canoes on ropes.

We passed Scoop Rapids after we had stopped to take out a supply of whitefish to eat, then on to Birch Portage, then Dog Portage, making slow progress. When we had reached Crow Lake (now named Corneille Lake), it was only six miles to a place where we would need to cut a two-mile portage. We would have to make a new freight road there to haul our fish from Jan Lake to join up with the winter freight road which ran from Flin Flon to Pelican Narrows.

We spent the first three days cutting out the old trapline trail that marked the portage; it had to be widened considerably to let horses and sleighs through. Then we began the large job of moving our outfit across this portage. We carried the big freighter canoe, now somewhat waterlogged, across in short stages. By the time we had made this portage, I had learned to pack with a tumpline, having at last developed my neck muscles to carry a good part of the load. It was easier than using a packsack, and I could carry more weight. Though my canoe had absorbed moisture into the wooden ribs and planking and now weighed eighty pounds, it seemed light, since I had become a better packer.

The route led across a small lake and ended at a four-hundred-yard portage. Here we again widened the trail for the winter freight road and at last came to the east shore of Jan Lake. We made our camp there that night, for there was a high wind blowing.

Awakened to bright sunshine and a light wind, we made a quick breakfast and departure. When we arrived at Sandy Island and our new fishing camp built that summer, every man was very happy indeed to have reached our destination.

When we put up our tent and unloaded our outfit, the date was November 1, 1931. Life took on a different pace now. Three weeks of paddling, portaging, and cutting roads had been a race against time. Afraid of becoming ice bound by freezing lakes and unsafe ice, we had worked from daylight until dark every day. Now the sun shone warmly and freeze-up was delayed, so we assumed a more leisurely pace and took time to enjoy our beautiful surroundings.

I wanted to build a hand-powered sawmill using the big rip saw that I had left in the cabin when it was built. With it, I planned to saw boards for the cabin floor. On a small island near the cabin, there stood a fine grove of white spruce. We built a scaffold there and squared two logs by hewing them with axes. I then marked them in widths of one and one-half inches. Using a fishing line and charcoal, I marked off the edge of each board. When we first tried out the saw, we had only succeeded in sawing two boards fourteen feet long before it was evening and time to quit for the day. The next day we sawed twenty-eight boards. The sawmill was operating satisfactorily as we changed off every fifteen minutes.

Then Bob and I left by canoe for Deschambault Lake to bring up the cookstove, stovepipes, sinkers and floats for the nets, all of which had been left at Tower Island the previous winter and now were required at our new location. We made this trip without any difficulty and returned just ahead of freeze-up. Then we made ready our fishnets for the fishing season, which would open on December 1.

My plan was for Bob and Harold to fish on Deschambault Lake to be ready for Chris Walker, who was coming up to get a load of fish for Nipawin. In case Walker wanted to come farther on to Jan Lake for big trout and whitefish, we cut out two portages of a mile long each. I hired two Indians to cut the portage between Deschambault and Pelican Lakes. Bob and Harold cut the other from Jan Lake to Pelican Lake before they left for their fishing station at Deschambault Lake. We hired Roderick Ballantyne to freight their supplies down with the dog team because by this time winter had set in. The fishing gear was already in camp for them, left there the previous season.

Soon, it was four days before the fishing season was to open. The men at Deschambault Lake jumped the gun a bit in sub zero weather when Fred Vessy arrived back from Lake Lenore. He was one of the fellows we had helped out when he came up in the previous winter with his inadequate fishing outfit. This time he had ten regular fishnets, various equipment, a helper, and a teamster with horses to take back a load of fish. He borrowed a ton of fish from our men to be paid back as soon as he could get his nets producing. In this manner, the teamster had a minimum of waiting time and left right away for civilization with his load.

Three days later, Chris Walker arrived at Deschambault Lake from Nipawin with two teams. Our lads had only one load of fish ready at that time. When Walker learned that it was only twenty-two miles to our Jan Lake operation, he took one team and an Indian guide and arrived at our camp in good order. He took a load of Jan Lake fish to Nipawin, the first such haul ever made to my knowledge.

At Deschambault Lake, our men fished until January 15, when a fight erupted between Vessy and his helper. They parted company, and the helper headed north with Harold Lowder, who wanted to quit fishing and go back to Flin Flon. Bob and Vessy would continue to fish at Deschambault, an arrangement that was entirely satisfactory to me.

Harold Lowder and Vessy's helper left for our Jan Lake camp carrying their bedrolls. They arrived at 9 P.M. after a very hard trip wading through heavy snow. The next day I paid Lowder his wages. He had $44 coming, and he said he was pleased, for it was more cash than he had seen in a long time. As it turned out, Lowder was the only man among us to make any money from that winter's fishing operation.

The very next day Bill James arrived with two teams to haul out fish to Flin Flon. Lowder and his companion left us then in the luxury of James' heated caboose, which he was using so that our fish was delivered to Flin Flon unfrozen.

That winter I was also trading for furs with the Indians and with a few white trappers that called in at our Jan Lake camp. I arranged to have freight brought in with the fish freighters. Our profit on trading was paying for our groceries. I traded one twenty-four hundred pound load of fish to Chris Walker for groceries and some cash. Trading in fact was a paying proposition. My buying price was eight dollars a hundred pounds for pork and five dollars a hundred for flour. Flour was selling for sixteen dollars a hundred pounds in Pelican Narrows. I sold mine for ten dollars. I doubled my money on all groceries and paid off nearly all our debt in Flin Flon.

We were not drawing on our fishing returns, leaving it all until spring so we would have cash when we returned to Flin Flon. At Flin Flon we had been promised eight cents a pound for whitefish. As our cost for fish boxes and freighting was three and one-half cents a pound, that would leave us a profit of four and a half cents. Our gross shipments to Flin Flon had been two hundred and forty-four boxes of fresh fish, on which we had expected to realize a profit of about four hundred dollars.

Near the end of the fishing season, I ordered twelve dozen muskrat traps and had them brought in with Bill James. I traded two dozen traps away and kept ten dozen. Then I sent word to Flin Flon that we would be in town about the end of May to collect the proceeds of our winter fishing. Bill James took back his two canoes on his last fish haul; after he left we were on our own.

Everyone at camp wanted to go muskrat trapping. Then Bob and Vessy pulled into camp from Deschambault Lake one day with Roderick Ballantyne, a native dog-driver who had bought all their supplies and equipment. These two fishermen were also eager to go trapping.

Now we were a group of five men once more, but the cabin was roomy and comfortable. We spent our time planning the coming muskrat trapping season, which was yet some weeks away, and operating our man-powered sawmill to cut some lumber. I had been a few boards short of completing the cabin floor, but now we cut twenty-eight boards extra and piled them so that they would season properly.

One day Fairburn said to me, "Olaf, I could make a canoe if I only had the material—canvas, paint, and nails."

Certainly another canoe would be a godsend for us with the muskrat season coming up. My own sixteen-foot canoe would prove most inadequate as soon as we had open water.

"Start building your canoe, Jim," I said. "I'll get Ballantyne to take me to Pelican Narrows with his dog team, so I can buy everything you need."

By the time I returned, Fairburn had sawn out two fine birch gunwales about sixteen feet long and several canoe ribs. He had spent time looking for just the right tree with the proper natural bend in it to form the curved ends of the canoe. He finally came up with a curved tamarack that he sawed in a neat cut that divided the trunk from end to end to form the desired canoe ends.

We all took a hand in the job. Some of us had a natural talent for working with wood, while others had learned from expert craftsmen. We also had the other canoe available to copy. Together we had the canoe ready for the canvas cover after one week. After keeping the hull in the cabin for three days, we applied the canvas, which was a tricky and exacting process.

The result was a fine birch canoe fourteen feet long and three-and-a-half feet wide. When after two weeks it was completed, with inside gunwales, centre cross bar and end thwarts, and a slick painted finish, it was as good as any factory-made canoe on the market at that time. I used that canoe for several years.

Then John Johnson and I left to begin trapping muskrats at Tulabi Lake,

Big Stone Lake, and the as-yet-nameless body of water that would in August 1935 be dubbed Hanson Lake. At that time, Side Lake had not been officially named either. Our plan was to return to Jan Lake via the Sturgeon-weir River at the end of the season. Fairburn and Vessy were to trap the Jan Lake area, while Bob would stay in camp and do some trading.

Roderick Ballantyne took my partner Johnson and me and our outfit across Jan Lake and the three-mile portage to Tulabi Lake on March 18, 1932. It was the first time I had trapped there. We had good luck and caught three hundred and fifty muskrats before moving on to Big Stone Lake. After a portage to Pasowun Lake, we camped overnight and caught only one muskrat. Next day we packed everything: fur, groceries, tent, stove, bedrolls, and canoe across the portage to Side Lake. This was prime muskrat country, but someone had been trapping there before breakup of the ice. We set all our traps in a creek running down to "my" lake.

I had a rough map made up for me by one of my Indian friends to guide me on this route. The lake was drawn with no detail and no outlet indicated. There we continued trapping.

By this time, we were almost out of groceries, with only five pounds of flour, a bit of sugar, and enough coffee to last for two weeks. There is a small creek flowing into the lake from Jack Pine Lake, and there we set up our camp. We made the short portage into Jack Pine Lake, where we were able to catch enough pickerel to keep us going. We spent our time trapping in this vicinity until the season ended.

Then we began to search for the outlet of the lake that would lead us to the Sturgeon-weir River. My Indian friend had not told me exactly where to look for the creek. A very irregular shoreline with long bays that led to dead ends further complicated matters. Striking southward from our last camp, we explored each bay, and it was easy going as long as we paddled south. We encountered strong head winds after we had reached the southern extremity of the lake without finding the outlet and had to turn northward to resume our search.

At the end of one bay, we found a small creek, but at its mouth there was no telling if the water flowed in or out. After paddling on this water-course for a few hundred yards, we found we were travelling upstream and therefore not on the outlet for the lake. Finally, wind-bound by high contrary winds we were laid up for two days, usually a depressing experience, but even more so when you are out of grub.

This trip was getting to John Johnson. New at the wilderness life, he seriously began to believe we were never going to find our way out of this lake and insisted that we return to Jan Lake the way we had come. I could see his point of view, since it did seem that this lake had no outlet at all. I explained to him, however, that the return trip via Tulabi Lake would be across thawing muskeg on one portage, a distance of three miles we had walked easily on our way in, but we would sink to our waists on a return walk.

My partner's mood grew worse. "You made a good job of getting the Indians to show you how to get into this lake, but you made a poor one of getting them to tell you how to get out," he growled.

I kept my peace. Among this labyrinth of bays, islands, and points, I was getting a bit concerned myself and hoped to find an out-flowing watercourse very soon. We worked our way northward until we were at the north-east end of the lake, where there are several islands. On the first island there stood a log cabin. No one was living there, but I had sensed we were near the outlet now. We travelled eastward with a fair wind, which took us to the east end of a bay in short order. Here at last we found a creek flowing generally south-eastward.

I tried to encourage him, but his black mood persisted and he refused to talk. I had learned from the Indians that there were four small portages on this creek, but since Johnson had elected to remain mute, I did not tell him of this fact. It was new country to us, and at a waterfall I missed finding the portage by looking for it on the wrong side. Johnson was good enough to help me let the canoe down a rope. Below the falls, we found the portage I had missed and a fine camping place. At this place we made a lunch of one small bannock, a bit of sugar, and black coffee.

At the fourth portage I told Johnson this was the last one. He looked at me as if to ask how I knew that. When we shortly reached the Sturgeon-weir, I believe he began to realize that I knew something about the country after all.

We travelled with a purpose now, going steadily upstream and over the portages we had cut to Jan Lake on our way in that previous autumn, arriving at the Jan Lake cabin in good condition, except that we were starving for good food.

Fairburn, Vessy, and Bob were in camp waiting for us. After two days of rest for all hands, we all left together for Flin Flon. Fairburn, Johnson, and I were in one canoe, while the two heavier men, Bob and Vessy, paddled the other.

Our first stop was at Pelican Narrows, where we had an offer of forty cents apiece for our muskrats. Johnson and I had four hundred and forty-eight skins, while Fairburn and Vessy had taken three hundred and ninety-seven. We had expected to realize fifty cents and so decided we could do better in Flin Flon.

In this thinking we were mistaken. Our final selling price was thirty-seven cents a pelt. My share of our catch was $82.88. Johnson however held his share until the next year, when he realized fifty cents a pelt. The rest of us had debts to pay, so had to sell and almost paid up in full with the proceeds.

Then we were off to see the fish buyer for our final settlement. There had been a hint that our proceeds might not meet our expectations; when Walker came for his last load of fish, he could pay only a cent and a half a pound, for the demand had fallen off. Still, we were hopeful, so the proceeds from the more than five tons we had shipped out that winter came as another surprise. Our buyer told us the fish had sold for an average of three cents a pound. We had originally been promised eight cents less freight and boxes totalling three and one half cents a pound, which would have left us four and a half cents net. At three cents a pound, the fish did not pay for the freighting, so we ended up in debt. I walked out of the office and swore to the boys that I would never, the rest of my life, go fishing commercially again.

9

JAN LAKE, 1932–33

THAT SPRING WHEN we passed through Pelican Narrows, the managers of both the Hudson's Bay Company and Revillon Frères trading posts had told us that, if we would spend from June to October at Jan Lake, they would pay us two dollars a month per dog to feed about forty company dogs. I had planned to do some work on the camp and then spend the off season prospecting, so I did not give the post managers a definite answer. Now the proposition looked good to us. At least it would be a living and since there was no return on the fishing operation, we were broke. I could not endure the thought of another hand-to-mouth summer in Flin Flon.

After three days Fairburn, Vessy, Bob and I decided to close the deal for feeding the dogs even though we would have to take our pay in trade at the stores in Pelican Narrows. The traders loaded forty dogs in five freighter canoes, and with two outboard motors towing their canoes and ours, made the twenty-five miles to our camp in four hours.

At that time the term for working dogs in the North was "sleigh dogs." It was not until dog team racing became popular as a sport that racing dogs became known as "sled dogs."

With an adequate supply of small steel cable we strung a line for each dog. One end was anchored to a tree and the other end to a stake driven a short distance out from shore into the sandy bottom. Each dog's chain was snapped into a sliding ring on the cable, which permitted the dog to exercise by running up and down the length of the cable, with access to water and to shade under the trees.

For a time the fishing was good and the dogs were well fed. After July 10, though, fishing dropped off so badly that we were using ten to twelve nets. Bob and I, who were responsible for feeding the dogs, did not have the easy time we had expected. We were kept busy washing our linen fishnets so they would not rot and then resetting them. Part of the time we fished with hook and line, trolling for large jackfish to assure enough fish to feed the dogs. This became a burden and just the opposite of the joy of sport fishing. Besides, the odour of decomposing fish in midsummer becomes oppressive. Two or three times a week we boiled fish to give the dogs a change, for there are always some dogs that do not thrive on a raw fish diet.

Another undesirable aspect of summer dog-feeding is that one is bound to his work. There can be no leaving the camp for any length of time for there are always dogs that get loose or tangled up one way or another. Only rush trips could be made to Pelican Narrows for supplies and never for more than one night away. But by September at least the fishing had improved so that it became considerably less work to feed them.

Fairburn and Vessy went prospecting in rocky country to the west of Jan Lake at a place called Poplar Lake. That summer they built a cabin to be their headquarters for trapping in the coming winter. Bob and I planned to trap out of the Jan Lake cabin.

That summer we lived on pickerel, bannock, and the corned beef "bought" at Pelican Narrows. Baking powder was used only for making bannock, our travelling ration. Since I did not like to use any more baking powder than was necessary, I also made sourdough bread and sourdough hotcakes. I shot one deer and we saved all the meat by digging a hole in a muskeg until we struck permafrost. We cut a hole in the frozen earth and lined it with moss to give us a cold storage vault. While we saw other deer swimming from island to island, they eluded us because, when fishing, we left the big game rifle at camp.

At this time we felled large birch trees and peeled off the bark to put on the roof of our cabin. We then laid poles over the bark slabs and covered the whole roof with a layer of clay. As long as I lived at Jan Lake that roof never leaked.

For another woodworking project, I bought a wrecked Gemini freighter canoe from an Indian who lived at Sandy Narrows. The canoe's planking had been badly broken, as were a number of its ribs, so the purchase price was only $5. Planking in a canoe is only one quarter of an inch thick. We ripped birch boards of this thickness on our sawmill to replace the damaged planking. The broken ribs were likewise replaced with sound new birch.

When the traders came back to pick up their dogs on October 5, Bob and I accompanied them to Pelican Narrows to pick up supplies. I obtained the necessary canvas and paint to finish the canoe repair job and on our return we went to work. We ended up with a fine freighter canoe.

With this craft we paddled to Flin Flon to buy sleigh dogs for use in our own winter trapping operation. In town I looked around until I located the pound. We had very little cash but I picked out two likely-looking dogs and paid one dollar apiece for them. I wanted one other dog that had just been caught but the pound keeper was adamant that I wait the regulation two days and if no owner showed up in the interval, I buy the dog at that time. I explained to him that by the time two days had elapsed we might well be frozen in and unable to return to Jan Lake by canoe. He finally compromised and sold me the dog for two dollars after a wait of one day.

We had our three dogs but no time to lose in getting underway. The Beaver Lake Road was passable at this time for nine miles out of Flin Flon as far as Loon Lake, where we had left our canoe. It was not necessary to hire a team for there was only our bedrolls and a few groceries to carry while we led our three dogs. With some scraps of meat that we had bought for a dollar to feed the dogs, we set out that night and arrived at Beaver Lake next morning.

A strong north-west wind was blowing so that we had to skirt the islands for shelter. Our big canoe was carrying a light load so that she rode the waves very well indeed and I was very happy that I had repaired it. After about twelve miles on an open stretch, we encountered great whitecaps. It was partly cloudy now and quite cold. We laid up on an island for the rest of the day, resuming our journey in the evening when the wind lessened. We made good time, but were so cold that I remarked to Bob, "It's a good thing that we must paddle so hard for that way we can keep warm. If we were using an outboard motor we would probably freeze to death."

It was a relief to get to the mouth of the Sturgeon-weir River and off the lake. There was no stopping at the settlement because other dogs were running at large that might attack ours. That night we camped at Spruce Portage where we gathered wood in the dark to make a campfire.

The dogs were on short rations as we were ourselves, having only coffee and some bread we had bought in town—all we could afford. We did have some flour, baking powder, and bacon that originally came with us from Pelican Narrows.

In making bannock I used shortening instead of lard and bacon fat instead of butter. Usually I made very thin bannock in the frying pan or "thick pancakes" as they were sometimes called. In winter I melted the shortening and used it to mix up my batter instead of using water. Bannock made in this manner can be chewed quite easily in severely cold weather, while bannock made with water is so hard at −40° Fahrenheit that it must first be thawed out at the campfire before it can be eaten.

Next morning our immediate destination was Scoop Rapids, there to obtain fish for the dogs and for ourselves. Our only obstacle was at Snake Portage where we dragged the canoe up the rapids by wading and pushing when the canoe could not be poled through the rocks. At the top of the rapid we quickly made a fire and put dry footwear on our freezing feet. The water was very cold, with skim ice in the backwaters and grassy shallows. In the afternoon the warm sunshine returned as did a fair wind that assisted us on our way to Scoop Rapids, where we arrived before dark.

Our first task was to catch fish for our dogs, and they were more than ready to eat the whitefish that we scooped out. After a big fish-fry for ourselves, we dressed forty whitefish for future use. The only container we could muster for the dressed fish was a canvas tarp.

We camped at Scoop Rapids that night, the only place on our travels where fish could be caught with a hand net. I would have liked to take a few hundred fish with us but there were still four portages to contend with on our way to Jan Lake and we were racing against the freeze-up once again.

The trip to Pelican Narrows took us two days because great seething whitecaps on Mirond Lake, brought by a gale blowing out of the north, kept us storm bound one day at Mirond Portage.

At Pelican Narrows we got traps and trapping supplies along with enough groceries to see us well into the trapping season. Fairburn and Vessy did not go to Flin Flon at all that fall but obtained their supplies on credit from Revillon Frères Fur Company as had Bob and I. We traded groceries to the natives for potatoes. I was bothered by the fact that all these supplies were charged to our accounts against the fur we had not yet caught. In those times most people were very cautious about going into debt.

A pleasant paddle of twenty-five miles in fine weather brought us back to the Jan Lake camp to complete the dog-buying trip to Flin Flon.

The canoeing season was extended by fine warm weather. Bob and I paddled to Deschambault Lake and brought back the dog harness and dog sleigh that I had left there two years previously.

Fairburn and Vessy were at our cabin when we returned. There was a good visit and everyone was in high spirits except for the spectre of a large debt hanging over our heads.

Bob had great plans for buying an outboard motor to power the big freighter canoe that I had repaired. I cautioned him thus, "We will be lucky if we can pay our debts this season. It would be better to wait and see if we have a surplus before we do anything like that."

One lucky day we found a great whitefish spawning ground where we kept fishing all night with one net until we had three thousand pounds of prime whitefish. We used the freighter canoe to haul our catch to the cabin in three trips. There they were dressed and hung ten to fourteen on a small pole run through a slash in the tail, so that they dried and froze to a cured state for dog food; enough for a long time.

Jan Lake froze over the first week in November. We trapped two foxes immediately. They were red foxes worth from ten to twelve dollars each. Later on, one coyote, three lynx, six mink, and four more foxes added to the original two only paid our debts because the price of furs was lower than we had expected. Again, supplies and groceries were taken against our chance of trapping more furs, now at large in the wilderness.

Bob, I said, "You can forget about buying an outboard motor. We are going to be lucky if we break even this season."

One day, a teamster by the name of White arrived at our Jan Lake Camp driving a team of greys. He had with him two fishermen, Ted Johnson and his helper. Johnson was going to fish on Deschambault Lake. They had brought a tent, an air-tight heater, and twenty nets. White turned out to be a fish buyer, and had brought a large number of fish nets for sale.

Everyone stayed in our cabin that first night. White was well known to Jim Fairburn and asked his whereabouts. I explained that Fairburn and his partner Vessy were at their trapping cabin at Poplar Lake some twenty miles from our camp. He said he would like to see Fairburn and have him go commercial fishing for him at Deschambault Lake.

I explained to White, "Fairburn and I are all through commercial fishing. We have lost money at it every time we tried it."

The next day White took Johnson and his man to Deschambault Lake. I gave him the key to my camp on Tower Island and told him he was welcome to stay there. Roderick Ballantyne showed up at this time to guide the fishermen to Tower Island.

White's venture failed miserably for the fishing was so bad that year that his men were catching only three or four fish to the net.

White did not give up easily. One day he returned from Flin Flon and came in to visit with me and enquired if I was aware of any other lake that might be good for commercial fishing. He had some maps of the Pelican Narrows district showing great detail. They had been made from aerial photographs; a kind of map I had never seen before.

This map proved my undoing for it was the bait to lure me back to commercial fishing. I had learned from the Indians that there were lots of lake trout in Mirond Lake and I told this to Mr. White. We pored over the map together that night by the light of a kerosene lamp. I saw that there were four portages from the north-east end of Jan Lake to Mirond Lake.

White was delighted. He asked me to bring all my fish nets, and he would sell me some more and we would set up a fish camp at Mirond Lake. Against my better judgement, I asked Bob if he wanted to go commercial fishing again.

"Well, trapping for fox, lynx, and coyote is about over for the season," Bob reasoned. We have enough fur to pay our debts and probably a credit by now, so let's go fishing."

The four portages were cut out in two days. I had taken a tent and fishing equipment, including two nets. After cutting test holes at a likely location in the ice of Mirond Lake and discovering a depth of sixty feet, we set the two nets as an experiment. To our knowledge this lake had never been commercially fished and was what fishermen called a "virgin lake."

Next morning, we were in for a surprise. The first net yielded twenty-two trout and the same number of whitefish. The second net had less trout but more whitefish.

When White received the news there began a scramble of activity. Ted Johnson, from Deschambault Lake, along with the Heinrich brothers who were back from the south, Gerald Bradley and the Booth brothers, Bob and I, all moved to Mirond Lake.

I picked out an island where our tents could be put up while some of us began to set nets. That day it began to snow. It was snowing heavily as we went to the main shore for firewood and it snowed hard until six inches of new snow had fallen. In the morning all trails had been filled with drifting snow. We set more nets in miserably cold windy weather.

One day we saw an aeroplane fly overhead on its way to Pelican Narrows.

The sighting of aircraft was tremendously interesting at that time, when aviation in the North was in its infancy. What interested us more was that on its return flight to Flin Flon, the plane touched down on the lake at our fishing camp. It bore the name "Arrow Airways, Flin Flon Manitoba" and the pilot was Jeff Home-Hay. He offered to freight our fish to Flin Flon. "I am hauling supplies to Pelican Narrows on a regular schedule, and we have made an agreement with Mr. White to freight out your fish as I return to Flin Flon," he informed us.

There was about four hundred pounds of trout and the same amount of whitefish on the ice ready to go. Home-Hay wanted fourteen hundred pounds and suggested he stay the night to get a full load.

To complete the load, we all started pulling nets that evening. Everything was ready by morning and Home-Hay took off, promising to return in three days for another load.

We went at the fishing with a will now, each man tending his own nets. Bob and I were doing well with our dog team and sleigh, hauling up to three hundred pounds of fish at a time. When the sleigh began to wear out I sent a note to White requesting a dog toboggan, and a sturdy oak toboggan arrived on the return flight. Our groceries were being delivered in the same fashion.

The fish catch continued to be good at Mirond Lake. It was not long before the word got around and soon four other outfits moved in and others followed later.

We all fished until March 15 when the season ended and everyone left for Flin Flon. I went out to settle with our fish buyer for our catch, while my partner Bob was flown out to the hospital at Flin Flon with pneumonia. He recovered in two weeks, but our partnership ended when he went to work as a trader for Revillon Frères.

The Booth brothers and Gerald Bradley flew out with the last load of fish but the rest of us were going to Flin Flon on foot. We made an early start with the dogs pulling our packs and bedrolls. Ted Johnson decided that he would walk at his own pace. The road was fine but when it grew dark we were still twenty miles away from our destination. Altogether we stopped three times for lunch and reached Flin Flon at about midnight.

While we expected Johnson to come in some time during the night, by morning he had not arrived. We became concerned and were considering harnessing up the dogs to go back and look for him but just before noon he walked into the Royal Hotel where we were staying.

Johnson explained how he had come to be detained. On Annabel Lake he had come upon open holes in the lake, two of them, about two feet in diameter. These holes are formed when heavy snow falls on the lake ice. The weight of the snow forces lake water up through a crack in the ice. When the water begins to flow it will melt a hole in the ice up to three feet in diameter. In the dark Johnson had fallen into one of them, the largest one. He went down to his waist, scrambled out, and ran to the nearby woods and lit a fire with the matches still dry in the breast pocket of his jacket, as was his tobacco. He kept busy for the rest of the night, cutting wood with his belt axe, just to keep warm and dry his clothing.

Ted Johnson left shortly for Lake Winnipeg and I never saw him again.

When I settled accounts with Mr. White, I received twelve dollars in cash for two months of hard work. Had I not bought the toboggan I would have had $28. We had been caught again by falling fish prices, and would have been much better off to have remained on the trapline. Fairburn and Vessy had done rather well trapping at Poplar Lake while we were freezing or worse at Mirond Lake. I promised myself again that this was the end of commercial fishing for me, but I had promised myself something like this at the end of previous fishing seasons.

Poor Bob had been laid low by pneumonia because he was a hard worker who got overheated out on the lake and then got chilled; common conditions when fishing with nets. When I think back of the hardships and cold of camping out by the fire, I wonder why I very seldom caught even a cold.

After spending two days in Flin Flon celebrating another bad fishing season, it was time to get busy and go spring trapping. When the Heinrichs brothers of the fishing crew wanted to go trapping I agreed, the proceeds to be split three ways. Then Gerald Bradley asked to go along. He had never set a trap in his life, having recently come from his parents' home near North Battleford. The four of us arranged that the Heinrichs boys would trap the north shore of Jan Lake and the east side, along with some small lakes to the north and the east of Jan Lake, using my freighter canoe. Fairburn and Vessy, I knew, would be trapping the west shore of Jan Lake from their Poplar Lake base. Bradley and I would use my dogs to haul my small canoe to Tulabi Lake to trap on the same route as had John Johnson and I in the previous spring.

White sent a team to Jan Lake to pick up his tents and fishing gear. We rode along on the sleigh and we met the Transport Freighting outfit returning from Pelican Narrows. They had left a good trail for us. The dogs followed along with an empty sleigh. Later we ran into heavy snow so that by the time we finally made it to the Jan Lake Camp we were tired of walking and of trying to find the trail on the ice.

We had a good rest. After a few days it turned so warm that the snow began to settle first and then the big melt began. Water pooled on the ice where deep snow had lain. Then it snowed lightly, turned cold enough to freeze the snow and water enough to carry the dogs and sleigh. I spent some days gathering my fishing gear and stowing it safely away in camp. I then took the tent, stove, and traps to Tulabi Lake, making the return trip in one day.

Bradley and I travelled to Pelican Narrows to buy groceries. Once again, we took these on credit to the fur trader against the furs we were going to catch. By now we were depending on the fur companies for our groceries, but I must say that we were treated fairly. Every time we went to Pelican Narrows, we spent a very pleasant evening playing bridge with the Revillon Frères post manager and his wife.

On Tulabi Lake the snow was melting fast. Bradley was getting experience trapping muskrats, but he did not like skinning and stretching the pelts. He turned out to be a fine companion and we enjoyed our trapping season—just the opposite of the trip I had made with Johnson a year earlier. Bradley was very good-natured. When an aeroplane passed by overhead, he declared, "Boy, I would sure like to be up there flying." I pointed out that he was right now having the time of his life. He was sitting in the canoe listening to the ducks quacking and the loons blowing the bugle. Finding a drowned muskrat in the next trap meant another fifty cents in your pocket, until after a few weeks you will be dreaming of muskrat pelts and fifty cent pieces rolling around.

That spring we portaged from Tulabi back to Jan Lake. This proved to be rough going indeed, through a place we called The Bog. It is three hundred yards across and if a packer steps in the wrong place he will sink to his hips. We made several trips across and Bradley proved himself an able packer.

The last half of the portage was high and dry. We felt as though we were walking along a highway in comparison to the first half.

By sundown we had packed all our freight to the Jan Lake shore. From where we sat drinking coffee, we could see our cabin on the island. Somehow this cabin always seemed like home to me, as it did for the other white trappers who made it their headquarters over the years.

We had a fine arrangement whereby as we gathered here in the spring we shared what foodstuffs we had left. Those who had run out of something got it from those who had it.

For several days we just rested and visited, talking about trapping experiences and wondering just how much we would make out of our spring hunt. Bradley and I had four hundred muskrat pelts for which we expected to get $200. One day an Indian arrived at camp and over an evening meal informed us that muskrats were selling at three pelts for a dollar at Pelican Narrows!

Then we took our furs to the Revillon Frères Fur Company in Pelican Narrows for we were under obligation to pay the debt we had incurred to grubstake the spring hunt. The manager counted our furs and offered forty cents each. Bradley and I received $165 and Fairburn and Vessy only $130. We all had some cash left after paying our bills, however, we would have no definite income until after the following November first when trapping season opened again.

10

THE WANDERING TRAPPERS

NOT A MAN AMONG US SEEMED to know what to do next. We sat around the fire one night and discussed our situation and all possibilities for making some money. Not that we were worried, for we could almost live off the land in the summertime, what with big game, fish and berries available, should our credit at the trading post be cut off. For that reason we could stay in camp all summer if we wished, and there are few places as good as Jan Lake in the summer time.

Bradley decided to return to Flin Flon for the summer. The Heinrichs brothers elected to stay at the Jan Lake camp for they had not even made enough money to visit their parents in Nipawin. Fairburn and Vessy would also stay.

On my travels to Pelican Narrows that summer I saw on the lake shore a derelict canoe—a big freighter with broken ribs and planking, its canvas rotting and falling away. It looked like something one would haul away to the dump. I enquired of the Indians there if the canoe was for sale. They had a good chuckle but directed me to an elderly Cree, the owner. He laughed outright when I asked him his selling price. Then he gladly accepted when I offered five dollars. I had come with my big canoe and I transported this wreck, top down across my gunwales, after the Indians had ballasted my own canoe with rocks to make everything more stable; then I paddled to the Jan Lake camp.

It almost seemed I would have to build a new canoe to repair this heap of rubbish. We spent some time looking it over. It had a square stern to accommodate an outboard motor, but we had none. It would be necessary to make all new gunwales, cross bars, a great deal of planking, front end, backboard, canvas, and twenty-seven ribs. Our man-powered sawmill was put to work, ripping out the boards. We all worked on the project, and with bolts and canvas brought in from Pelican Narrows, completed the job in short order. Our canoe was as good as a new one for a cash outlay of twenty dollars.

Later the Heinrichs brothers bought a wrecked eighteen-foot freighter. We were all experienced canoe builders by this time and put this canoe into first class condition. Then a third canoe, a sixteen-foot prospector model was acquired for repair during the coming winter. We felt a little proud of these accomplishments and happy that we were now so well supplied with canoes.

I had become interested in prospecting. For some time I had wanted to look for minerals in the region but I did not get the opportunity that summer. I made several trips alone into the hills around Jan Lake but found nothing of interest.

The Heinrichs brothers that summer bought four pups from an Indian. They ran loose all summer at camp and grew large enough to work when winter came. I made a trip to Flin Flon with Bob, my last year's partner, who now worked for Revillon Frères. At the dog pound we haggled with our old friend the pound keeper and came away leading five big friendly dogs bought for a total of thirty dollars. Two were for me to round out my team to four good dogs and the other three were Bob's.

On that trip when I purchased groceries I found that our debt was over $200. This caused the Heinrichs brothers such concern that they voiced the opinion that if the bottom should drop out of the fur market then we would owe $500 by spring.

We did have a good catch of fur that winter; several foxes and coyotes, five lynx, and some mink. By Christmas, our bill had been paid at Pelican Narrows and we even had some credit on the books. The brothers bought a dog toboggan and harness. Fairburn and Vessy relied on the two dog teams at camp for their freighting needs. There was considerably less hardship that winter than any of the winters I had gone commercial fishing and had wound up without food and clothing. That was one winter when I kept my promise never to fish again.

Towards spring we were repairing canoes again. The last canoe purchased in the fall was fully repaired. Then Roderick Ballantyne brought in the worst wreck yet. This pile of junk was so dilapidated that I hunted for a long time to find a tree with just the proper shape to cut out two new ends for the craft. This canoe too we put in first class condition.

Once more we prepared to go trapping muskrats. That season Fairburn and Vessy trapped the south and east shores of Jan Lake. Fred Heinrichs worked the north end of that lake, used the main cabin, and fed the dogs. Bob Heinrichs and I would cover Tulabi Lake and eastward.

With two canoes now, Bob Heinrichs and I covered a great deal of territory and finished the season with over five hundred pelts. Fred Heinrichs had more than two hundred. We realized seventy cents a skin in that spring of 1934.

That year we bought two Johnson one-and-one-half horsepower motors for $115 each.

When we arrived in Flin Flon that spring the miners had gone on strike for higher wages. That meant that all the beer parlours were closed. Only the bootleggers were in operation and whiskey sold for fifty cents a swallow and beer was two bits for a small glass. I did not buy any drinks as I never was a serious drinker at any time. Not so were some of the trappers in town to celebrate. It was sad to see them spending their hard-earned money on bootleg booze.

On our way back to Jan Lake we camped at the Indian village of Birch Portage. All the men were there having just arrived home from far-away traplines. They were interested in one of our canoes—one that I had almost totally rebuilt. One man asked me what price I would take for it.

"Oh," I said, "I guess it ought to be worth $25."

He ran to his cabin and brought out the cash—five ones and a twenty dollar bill.

There was nothing I could do but load everything in that craft to one of our other canoes.

On our return trip to Pelican Narrows, we had brought in thirty-five hundred pounds of freight to the Revillon Frères trading post there. For this we were paid four dollars a hundredweight or $140 for the trip. With outboard motors to drive our big canoes this had been a good earning, which was divided between five of us. This also paid for our travelling expenses to Flin Flon.

Fairburn, Vessy, and Bob Heinrichs left Pelican Narrows for our camp at Jan Lake, taking the dogs which had been left in the care of an Indian. Fred Heinrichs and I, in company with the Revillon trader and a native guide named David Mirasty, then freighted three Revillon canoes loaded with supplies to the south end of Reindeer Lake.

Mirasty was extremely capable and a strong packer. The water was so high that summer that at all the rapids the water had backed up into the trees. The flood had spilled over the banks of rivers and the shores of lakes so that trees standing in water became a common sight. Mirasty said it was thirty years since the water had been so high. We avoided a great deal of portaging; at some of the rapids we pulled up the canoes by hand among the trees, wading waist deep in water. At larger rapids only part of the loads were portaged, the partly loaded canoes were pulled up through flooded and seldom used channels, now become navigable. Mirasty knew exactly where to go at all times and we lost no time by never having to backtrack and look for the route.

This was my first trip to Reindeer Lake and it was certainly an interesting journey. At Frog Portage the water was pouring over the bank of the Churchill River, over the divide and into Wood Lake, which is part of the Saskatchewan River drainage basin. When this occurs the water level rises about six feet on the Sturgeon-weir River and even Beaver Lake had been known to rise high enough to inundate the docking facilities and boat houses.

With two outboard motors to push us along, the trip was made in one week. We cleared about $20 each for our work.

On our return to Jan Lake the Heinrichs brothers left for Nipawin by canoe, a long journey by way of Sturgeon-weir River and Cumberland Lake, then upstream on the Saskatchewan River.

A great change had taken place for us since the acquisition of the outboard motors. It was now possible to travel against the wind and sit back in our good canoes and just watch the shoreline recede into the distance. I sold my nineteen-foot freighter to a trapper for $90. I traded my smaller canoe for a twenty-foot freighter so that I could haul a larger load. This canoe needed a new canvas which I applied for a cost of $20. Then I made another freighting trip for Revillon Frères with two Indians. This time we went to Flin Flon and again cleared $20.

Fairburn and Vessy remained at Jan Lake all summer. They did some prospecting and I accompanied them on several trips into mineralized areas. We worked at a spot where we hoped to find gold, but discovered nothing of commercial value there. We were hampered in travelling any distance in that we had to feed the eight dogs at camp.

That summer too I began to concentrate on adding to my woodcraft knowledge by making a study of trees and other vegetation to assist me in my wilderness travels. I received my finest training in direction sense while at Jan Lake. Prospecting was working handily into this study and I was improving in my ability to find my directions. I have known Indians who got lost and had to face real hardship. Of course, white men were reported lost every year in this country and some were never found where they lay dead of starvation and exposure. As time went on I never had any difficulty in getting back to camp. The signs had become very plain indeed. By watching these signs closely and making a mental note of each time I changed my direction while walking in the bush as you often do while prospecting, I could always point back to camp with accuracy. I also knew how far I was from camp. After two years of this study any time I was in the woods, in sunshine, cloud, fog, rain, or snowstorms, I always knew how to determine my location in relation to my starting point. It grew to be a real pleasure to confidently strike out on foot through new country.

Today Jan Lake is a popular summer resort and a great place to spend a vacation. The scenery is uncommonly beautiful with its many islands with fine sandy beaches. As I think back on my years at Jan Lake I realize it was one of the most pleasant times of my life. There were hardships of course, but there were many compensations.

We had no worries. Every day there was something new to be done and new projects were always being planned. Each time someone went to Pelican Narrows he brought back our mail along with newspapers and magazines. We wore out many decks of cards. In our first year at Jan Lake I bought a gramophone and many additions to my record album collection. When we finally got tired of hearing the same tunes I traded gramophone and records away to an Indian.

Early in September the Heinrichs brothers returned from Nipawin. They had made a very fine voyage by canoe, five days to their destination and the same on the return trip. From Nipawin they had freighted two hundred pounds of flour, fifty pounds of sugar, one hundred of potatoes, and two sides of bacon. Prices of these items in Pelican Narrows were almost double their cost outside.

On September 10, 1933, we all left for Flin Flon to purchase what we needed before trapping began once more. I met Jack Hackens, who wanted to join me because he had not been taken back as an employee after the mine strike was settled. I agreed to take him along if he would pay his share of the expense, a proposition to which he readily agreed.

Once more we were a group of six, commonly known around Flin Flon as "The Jan Lake Trappers."

On our return trip when we called in at Pelican Narrows, the post manager for Revillon Frères hired the six of us to build a bunkhouse to accommodate overnight guests. We all pitched in and had the cabin built in eight days—a neat little structure of peeled logs, factory windows, and "Rubberoid" roofing. Small logs had been hewn square and placed side by side over the dirt to make a fine solid floor.

It was nearing the end of September and that time of the year when we should have been on our way to prepare for the trapping season. In spite of this, the post manager talked us into staying two more days when an aeroplane was due in from Flin Flon. Aboard would be a supply of liquor with which we could all celebrate the completing of the bunk house—a kind of bunk house warming as it were.

When the plane at last arrived we all trooped down to the dock. The pilot confirmed that the liquor was aboard indeed. The first thing we did was to offer him a drink, which he declined, saying that were he not obligated to continue his flying schedule that day, he would certainly have stayed and helped us to celebrate.

In the liquor shipment there were three bottles of Scotch whiskey, three bottles of rye, two gallons of wine, and two cases of beer. The manager took one bottle of Scotch and a case of beer. The balance was for the celebration.

I will always remember that particular evening. The plane had arrived quite late in the day when we were in the process of preparing our supper. Two freighters with two loaded canoes arrived just after dark, followed shortly thereafter by two trappers just arrived from Ballantyne Bay. One was a white man, the other a native. We had finished our supper when they arrived.

The last two arrivals went up to the store, bought some grub for supper, came back to the bunkhouse and started frying some corned beef. When we offered them a drink they accepted gladly. They looked tired and half starved from their long trip on short rations. They both took a big drink of whiskey and very soon began to show its effects. We passed each a big slug of wine and then a bottle of beer apiece. They had forgotten about eating and one mumbled something about paying for their share of the booze.

"Forget it," someone sang out. "This is on the bunk house."

The corned beef was burnt black before they got around to looking at

The beaver won't rise to Hanson's bait.

it. One of the trappers took a bite but the other was sitting on the floor, unable to stand up.

The two freighters came over to join the celebration. They also each took a big drink of whiskey, a cupful of wine, and a bottle of beer.

Fairburn had taken only one drink of whiskey and that before supper. I had stopped drinking when I saw what was happening. I saw Fairburn silently pick up his sleeping bag and walk out in disgust to find a quiet place to sleep. I did not see him again that night.

When the manager came over to see us some of the men were staggering about or holding onto something for support, while others were crawling around on their hands and knees. He talked for a while about good times and hard times, took a few drinks and then left.

The two freighters were standing near a window. One pushed the window open, leaned across the sill and proceeded to vomit the whiskey, wine, beer and his supper for the whiskey jacks to look over in the morning. The other fellow decided that he did not have time to make it to the door either so he jumped up on his partner's back, hung his head out the window and was sick also.

No one had mentioned that he was hungry. One of the Ballantyne Bay trappers managed to pick up his sleeping bag and walk out. His partner, who had earlier begun to cook supper, was now sound asleep in the middle of the floor. Fred Heinrichs and I pulled him over to a wall and out of the way. The two freighters left then; one leaning against the other as they staggered down to their canoes. By 2 A.M. only the Heinrichs brothers and I were left in the cabin and turned in for the rest of the night.

Next morning most of the men were badly hung over and there was very little liquor left. Fairburn, the first man to get up, and I, who had soon followed, were enjoying the sight of all those trappers and canoe freighters greet the day, some sitting up and others still in their bedrolls. The new bunkhouse had been officially opened.

It was after dinner before our group got underway for Jan Lake. We left in pairs, two men to a canoe with Fairburn and Vessy in the lead, the Heinrichs brothers followed, while Jack Hackens and I were last to leave. It was dark when we got 'home' as we always referred to the Jan Lake cabin. Here we were safe from outside influences and here we could find peace, contentment, and rest.

The next morning we went across to the west shore where we had left our dogs and fish nets with Roderick Ballantyne, who had agreed to feed the dogs in our absence. He complained that he had had great difficulty in catching fish to feed our dogs and his own. We paid him off in groceries which left him a much happier man.

It was mid-October and time to put up fish for dog food. Hackens and I set up a tent on the south shore of Jan Lake as a base camp for fishing. That day Hackens suddenly asked me if I knew what the date was.

"I think it must be the 14th of October," I suggested.

"Well no. It is actually the 13th and that's bad luck," he said gravely.

The first time we looked at the net we counted thirteen fish, also a bad luck sign, according to Hackens. Multiples of thirteen were just as unlucky, he said. In spite of these omens of misfortune we all had a good winter. When Hackens and I caught twenty-six foxes he thought it a bad sign for we had thirteen apiece and should catch more to break the evil sign. We did not catch another fox that winter.

Altogether, Hackens, the Heinrichs brothers and I collected forty foxes, twelve coyotes, six lynx, thirteen mink, and several weasels. Prices for fox were from ten to fifteen dollars a pelt, coyote averaged eight dollars, lynx forty, and weasel one dollar. We had made wages at least, splitting the proceeds four ways.

We looked forward now to the opening of the muskrat trapping season. On our travels that winter we saw hundreds of muskrat houses any time we were in an area where there were bulrushes and reeds along the shores of lakes and rivers. In fact the country was full of muskrats according to all the signs.

In March the traps were set. Strangely, as we opened the muskrat dens many were found to be frozen up, in fact, dead muskrats in some of their houses, frozen solid and shrouded in hoar frost. Hackens and I worked the Tulabi Lake area while the Heinrichs brothers trapped on Jan Lake. Hackens and I caught eighty muskrats while the brothers gathered about one hundred. Fairburn and Vessy came over one day with the disquieting information that very few live muskrats were to be found in their trapping territory.

Something very strange had happened. Where there were large numbers of muskrats last fall, now there were only a few or none at all. We came to the conclusion that some sinister disease had severely decimated their numbers, probably the same that kills off bush rabbits every time their numbers reach a certain level in relation to the amount of winter food available in that area.

Fred and Bob Heinrichs then came up with the news that while travelling through the channels and marshes of the Cumberland Lake region on their return from Nipawin they had observed muskrats swimming everywhere, more than they had ever seen before.

Our plans for further spring operations were considerably revised at this time. Four of us would move south-eastward some sixty miles as the crow flies to the Cumberland country to trap muskrats. Following generally the creeks and lakes, that distance would stretch to one hundred miles. Fairburn and Vessy would take their small canoe down to where Hackens and I had already hauled our freighter canoe on Tulabi Lake. Bob and Fred were to stay at Jan Lake and trap as many muskrats as possible on the ice before following us with their big canoe and outboard motor later in the season. On their way they were to trap Tulabi Lake in open water, then Tulabi Brook to Bigstone Lake, down to Grassberry River, then rendezvous with us at Windy Lake to wind up the trapping season.

The advance party, Fairburn, Vessy, Hackens and myself chose a partly overland route westward of the Heinrichs' route, through lakes, muskeg, and swamp. Once we reached Brougham Creek, we would canoe down to Mossy River, and then down to Cumberland Lake. On our return we would meet the Heinrichs brothers by ascending the Grassberry River to Windy Lake. All our planning had been done from a recently completed aerial map of the region.

Our advance party left Jan Lake as scheduled, with the dogs transporting our gear, supplies, and canoes. This involved more than one trip to haul everything across the still frozen lakes and the portages. We stopped for a time at Big Stone Lake where only three muskrats were taken. As we moved along, we had set traps then returned to pick them up when we backtracked to bring up our freight in relays. Later we tried trapping at Limestone Lake but found all the muskrat houses and push-ups to be frozen solid. This was a week out of Jan Lake.

The travelling had been very good until our route led southward and we had to cut a mile long portage to an unnamed lake we had seen only on the map. Here we counted about fifty muskrat houses, which motivated us to set up our tent and begin trapping. Meanwhile, I made two trips back to our last camp and hauled up the canoes. The snow was disappearing more each day now as the warming sun shone brightly every day. This heat would put an end to sleighing any day now.

The trapping results at this lake were so poor that we moved on. Once again we found frozen muskrat in houses everywhere.

We still had a half-mile portage to cut before we struck the headwaters of Brougham Creek and our water route to Cumberland Lake. The snow was all gone, which forced us to drag everything or carry it across that portage. The dogs gave us great deal of assistance for they worked hard dragging the sleigh and small loads over the trail while being fuelled on boiled corn meal.

In the grassy upper reaches of Brougham Creek it was now spawning time for jackfish and suckers, so dog food was easily available. We caught the jack for ourselves and suckers, which we boiled, for the dogs.

A fine camping spot was found where there was much dry firewood. After a week it was time to move on but the creek was so full of fallen trees that canoeing was impossible. We cut a portage through tamarack swamp and moved all our gear to a place on the creek where it ran through open muskeg and a large swamp.

This turned out to be the most difficult canoe trip that I have ever made. It took us six days to travel one section of Brougham Creek to the point where it joins the Mossy River, a distance of seven miles cross country. In places the creek's channel was so choked with willows that we had to chop a channel to get our canoes through.

One morning as I was standing in the canoe I saw a large lone tamarack about a quarter of a mile to the south.

I said to Fairburn, "I hope that we can reach that tree by lunch time so that we can have our lunch on dry ground."

After four hours of travelling I realized that we would not be lunching at that spot. We were a little closer but the creek was so crooked that we were travelling in all directions to follow its course. There was a great deal of water moving with the spring thaw in what was normally a small meandering stream. We waded, often up to our hips at some spots, while pulling the canoes along. In some places the water was over the banks so that at one point we waded the canoes into the open swamp to get around dense willow growth in the creek bed. In many very sharp bends we had to the lift the canoes at their sterns to pass dense clumps of willow.

All the while the creek was swarming with spawning fish. As we waded on, we saw fish in the creek ahead of us and in the grass along the banks. Dog feeding was even easier now for the fish were so thick that the dogs caught them themselves. We obtained fresh fish for our own food by clubbing them with our paddles.

The dogs, of course, could not travel in the canoes for we were forever lifting the craft to get them farther downstream. Thus the dogs ran free, having a wonderful time fishing, or just cavorting in the water.

Sometimes we would not see them for an hour or more. Then they came charging back with tongues lolling and spray flying to find us and a dry place to lie down and rest.

At intervals of about an hour it became necessary to clean out the canoes. As we had dragged our canoes around the sharp bends, dry branches, moss, and other debris fell into them so that they took on the appearance of two large crows' nests.

The only way to get to dry land on this creek was to wade the canoes out of it, across the bordering swamp, and into the trees. We saw many muskrat feeding stations but did not set traps because we could not get back to them with canoes.

After the sixth day of this travel at a snail's pace, the creek suddenly widened and we resumed normal paddling. Hackens and I caught five muskrats in this area. Meanwhile, Fairburn and Vessy had taken nine more while working farther downstream. These were the last muskrats our party took in these waters.

At this time one of my dogs became very sick. Sadly I had to part with it and buried the carcass covered with moss in a muskeg. I never learned the cause of its problem.

At long last we were on the Mossy River. The current was so swift that travel was brisk over fast-flowing water in the shallows and in the navigable rapids. When we came to the end of the swift water we stopped to skin and dry our most recently caught muskrats. Our grand total was twenty-six since leaving Jan Lake.

While our group was camped there two men came paddling upstream in a canoe and stayed to a visit. When they learned that we had come all the way from Jan Lake to trap muskrats in the Cumberland country they both began to chuckle.

One said, "You might as well take it easy and have a good rest. We have not caught a single muskrat in the past week. There are no muskrats to be seen anywhere on Cumberland Lake or the Saskatchewan River. Right now we're on our way up the Mossy River to trap muskrats."

Nature had used its own ruthless method of solving the problem of the great abundance of muskrats. A disease I considered might have been water-borne accounted for the many hundreds of dead muskrat houses we had seen.

We thought about accompanying our two visitors up the Mossy River but we were too many trappers for the available fur. Instead we decided to ascend the Saskatchewan River to the Old Channel in search of muskrats. As we started on our way we met a lone trapper returning from the Old Channel. He told us that he had been trapping there for four days and had caught but two muskrats.

There was nothing else we could do but turn back. At the mouth of the Grassberry River in those days stood a trading post called Pine Bluff. Our twenty-six muskrat pelts sold there for $1.30 each. After a stay of two days we pointed the canoes northward and upstream on the Grassberry River.

While we had travelled in the Cumberland region our outboard motor had been put to work. After replenishing our gas supply at Pine Bluff, I was towing the other canoe. Past three miles we found shallow water that put an end to travel by motor. The river was so shallow in several places that we waded the canoes. In stretches of deep water we could paddle.

After a day and a half we reached Windy Lake. Here the motor could be used once more and with the greatest of pleasure. After crossing Windy Lake we headed for Suggi Lake. On the river that connects the two lakes, we saw a campfire on the bank, and drawing closer we were surprised and delighted to find the Heinrichs brothers waiting for us.

They were relieved for they had been waiting for three days and were about to go down to Pine Bluff to make enquiries about our whereabouts. As we compared notes we learned that they had, since we parted, caught fifty-seven muskrats, most of them before they left Jan Lake. Ruefully we all admitted that the muskrat hunt of the spring of 1935 had been a disaster. Once our pelts had been traded away at Pine Bluff there was a surplus of only ten dollars to be divided between the four men of the advance party.

Across country it is not far to Flin Flon, probably thirty-five miles. Our entire group ascended Balsam Creek to Little Limestone Lake (Usinne Lake). We spent two days on the shallow creek wading or dragging the canoes over shallows and beaver dams. The next day a portage of three quarters of a mile brought us to Balsam Lake. A short portage saw us on the shore of Beaver Lake. Everyone was happy to be so near to Flin Flon.

It was the third day since leaving Windy Lake. Fairburn was at this time appointed camp cook while some of us set a fishnet. That night it caught five whitefish for us and one sucker—a slim meal for the dogs in camp, now numbering seven since the Heinrichs' had brought their four from Jan Lake.

Once across Beaver Lake the next day we camped at the mouth of Meridian Creek. There were enough muskrat signs there to persuade us to resume trapping. The Heinrichs brothers elected to move on up Beaver

Lake, as they intended to portage to Mosher Lake on an alternative route to Flin Flon.

Fairburn, Vessy, Hackens and I began to set traps upstream on Meridian Creek as we worked our way closer to town. After five days of trapping we headed for Flin Flon with twenty-eight muskrats.

On our way we reached Bootleg Lake and the site of the Henney-Malone Mine. This mine had closed when the ore supply was found to be insufficient to warrant its continued extraction.

Mr. and Mrs. Henney still lived there. They asked us to have supper with them that night. We had a most delicious meal and spent a wonderful evening. Our conversation centred around mining, prospecting, and trapping. Henney enquired if we had ever seen in all our travels any good gold or copper showings. I explained to him that I had trapped on a good sized lake, as yet unnamed, which looked very promising for copper and gold—a bit of information in which he showed keen interest.

We slept in their bunkhouse that night and the next morning went down to the lake shore to cook breakfast.

Henney came along and insisted that we eat breakfast in his home. He wanted to know what we were doing for the summer and I told him that we were dead broke and at loose ends. He then proposed that we go prospecting, he to furnish the groceries and gasoline for my outboard motor in exchange for a fifty-fifty split on any profit. We all accepted except for Hackens, who wanted to try to get his job back in Flin Flon.

The Henneys agreed to look after my dogs and our canoes while we walked to Flin Flon, where we sold our furs for $35. With the proceeds we did some shopping in town for summer clothing and a few necessities for prospecting.

Here we met the Heinrichs brothers for the last time. Sometime on their way to Flin Flon they had suddenly changed their minds and gone north to Pelican Narrows. There they sold their four dogs for $20; toboggan and harness went for $8. They had travelled on to Jan Lake and picked up all their possessions at the cabin. Then they sold all their traps to Revillon Frères Fur Company. The brothers still had their canoe and outboard motor for sale. They were going to live in a shack with Hackens while they tried to get work at the mine.

I heard later that they were unsuccessful in finding employment at the mine and that Bob Heinrichs returned to his home at Nipawin. Fred Heinrichs moved eastward to Sudbury, Ontario and went to work at the nickel mine where he did well, got married, and bought a good home. Jack Hackens went to live in England. All left in the summer of 1935.

Just before I left Flin Flon I sold my dogs for $35 to two trappers from Reindeer Lake who were just arrived in Flin Flon to sell their furs. I kept my dog harness and dog sleigh as an ace-in-the-hole should I some day need to return to trapping as a livelihood.

Hanson the prospector, circa 1935.

11

NO POT OF GOLD

During the summer of 1935 Jim Fairburn, Fred Vessy and I left Henney-Malone Mine for that as-yet-unnamed body of water which would become known as Hanson Lake. We had finalized our agreement with Mr. Henney to prospect this area. Full of enthusiasm that we would be the first prospectors to search this part of the wilderness for minerals, we descended Meridian Creek with two canoes and reached Beaver Lake.

Our cargo, besides the usual grubstake and equipment, included such unusual items as one case of dynamite and two jack hammers, a forge, a small anvil, a bag of coal, and a blacksmith's hammer for sharpening steel; all supplied by Henney as part of the deal. I also had a borrowed book on prospecting so that every time we picked up some mineralized rock I could check it in the book.

I was realizing my dream of long standing, a dream to prospect that part of the country, a dream that had grown ever since I had first seen it when travelling with John Johnson back in 1932.

I towed the small canoe that belonged to Fairburn and Vessy across Beaver Lake and up the Sturgeon-weir River to where it is joined by the creek that drains Hanson Lake. As we entered this watercourse we found the water level to be very low due to scanty rainfall all that summer. Arriving at shallow rapids the water ran only a few inches above the rocks, and here we found a man-made channel where someone had removed the rocks to let his canoe pass through. Some rocks bore green paint from a canoe that had been dragged over them and we were leaving blue paint from ours. When we found fresh boot tracks on the very first portage we could tell that their owners were carrying heavy loads. We knew that when we got to the lake someone would already be there.

On reaching the main part of the lake we headed for shore to make camp at a good spot among the jack pines. After the tent was set up we made a table and two benches for our use while we stayed here for the next few days. The afternoon was spent searching the hills for mineral but on our return, and while preparing for the night, we heard two dynamite blasts. It was certain that we were not the only prospectors at work on the lake.

We knew too, that these unknown men had arrived just ahead of us and our chances of making a strike were every bit as good as theirs.

The next day we were prospecting at the north-east extremity of the lake where Fairburn and Vessy found a good-sized body of heavy mineral. There was no rust, and the rock was a stable blue-black colour.

"What kind of mineral is it?" I asked Fairburn excitedly.

"I think it has to be iron ore," he said. "I have seen a lot of iron but this is different because there is no rust on it anywhere."

Some time was spent looking over the find while we gathered about twenty-five pounds of samples and transported them back to camp.

That day we heard only one blast and were intending to visit our fellow prospectors on the following day. However, as we were having breakfast the next morning they arrived in sight, travelling fast in their motorized canoe. When they saw us they changed course, beached their canoe, then came up and introduced themselves as Oliver Walker and Anson Erickson, on their way to Flin Flon to have their samples assayed.

After a short conversation we offered them coffee and then the five of us sat around the table and talked.

"Have you had any luck?" I asked.

They were all smiles and in the best of humour. Walker went over to his canoe and hauled out a bag containing about a hundred pounds of samples.

"Take a look at that," he said happily as he went back to his coffee.

Fairburn, Vessy and I gathered around the bag. Fairburn, veteran prospector that he was, examined a piece carefully, turning it over slowly while studying it from all angles.

"Galena," Fairburn announced, "Galena—silver and lead, solid galena, the whole damned bagful! "

There were two more bags of ore in the canoe.

Walker was an old timer at the prospecting game. He told us that he had prospected in British Columbia for many years. Now he excitedly informed us he had struck it rich for the first time in his life. These men were very anxious to be on their way and we were soon waving good-bye to two very happy prospectors.

Disappointedly I told my partners that I should have prospected this lake back in 1932 and now it was too late. We paddled over to where Walker and Erickson had staked their claims and studied the trench they had blasted to obtain their samples. Then we went back and studied the blue-black ore we had found. We decided to stake some claims on our find as our new acquaintances had done on theirs.

The staking of claims began the next day. Fairburn tried to run the lines using a compass but he found it to be useless because the needle pointed in all directions. Fairburn knew then that we had iron magnetite. I read in the *Prospector's Handbook* that this ore sometimes contains gold and other rare minerals. Our hope was that we had something of good value. We resumed staking by using the sun for a guide, until six claims had been staked there.

Next we decided to ascend a small creek on the west side of this lake to prospect at two small lakes nowadays called Bad Carrot Lake and Side Lake. However, on the night before we left Hanson Lake, Fairburn had had a vivid dream that there existed a very rich copper mine on a birch and poplar covered island in Hanson Lake. When he told me about this I assured him that there was indeed such an island in this lake, in fact, this island lay alongside our course to Side Lake. When we came to the east end of the island I asked Fairburn, "Does this island look like the island of your dreams of the copper mine?"

"Well it does have birch and poplar, just as in my dream," he admitted.

I suggested that we prospect the island but Fairburn would have no part of it, stating that he put no stock in dreams. At least I got him to run the outfit slowly to the far end of the island while Vessy and I walked the shore, one on each side to do a bit of observing, but we found no mineral.

Fairburn and Vessy travelled together while prospecting while I took to the trail alone. One day as I was working near two small lakes near the north side of Side Lake and on one of my old trapline trails, I came upon a place where squirrels had been digging up something that looked like white salt. After examining this substance closely and digging up more of it I discovered that this was almost pure silica sand. With my prospector's pick I dug several small holes and found that the silica deposit was spread over a wide area. I took a sample back to camp where, we felt (with the usual prospector's enthusiasm) that we were in on a fortune. Next day we went back and dug a hole seven feet deep, but did not find bottom in the soft white sand. By this time we were convinced that we were as well off as Walker and Erickson who had struck it rich at Hanson Lake.

Of course we staked claims on the silica sand deposit. We also staked a mineral showing nearby where we had found a high rusty hill containing iron pyrites good for six claims.

At this time we made ready to return to Flin Flon with all our samples to have them assayed. One nice day everything was loaded into the canoes and we set out on our way from Side Lake. When crossing Hanson Lake and as we passed "The Island of the Copper Mine Dream" we saw that the entire island had been staked in our absence. We stopped and I went over and read the staker's name on one of the stakes. It was Stanley Simpson of the consolidated Mining and Smelting Company. At the far end of the island we found two tents and two men having tea. We stopped in for a chat, and they turned out to be Simpson and his helper. They showed us some fine copper ore samples and took us to a trench where we looked at a very good copper showing.

Fairburn, I noticed, was doing a lot of thinking at this time, as Vessy and I were doing also as we continued on our way. I know that all three of us regretted deeply that we had not followed that dream and prospected the island covered with birch and poplar. There is no doubt that we would have made the copper find as it was right on the surface where anyone could have seen it. From a distance it looked like a great patch of rust. I had asked Simpson for a sample which he graciously provided, along with a cup of tea all around before we departed.

At the site of our first camp we now wanted a cache in which to store some of our equipment until we returned for more prospecting. In a place where four tall trees stood close together, we built a ladder eighteen feet long, then wired poles crosswise to the trees and about fifteen feet above the ground. We cut the tree tops so that the wind would not rock the trees and wear them loose from their wire bindings. Then a platform was built over the poles, the equipment placed on it, and a tarp lashed over the entire lot.

On this trip we had come too late for the galena deposit and we had missed by a whisker the staking of the copper showing on the island. Vessy and I asked Fairburn never to pass up a dream again.

All we had to bring to Mr. Henney was magnetite iron and silica sand. Henney took the magnetite to the assay office in Flin Flon where it tested 68 per cent iron without a trace of gold. The sand had to be sent to Ottawa for a government assay, where it tested 99 4/10 per cent pure. It would be worth $25 a ton laid down at a glass factory, but that time it would have cost that amount to get it to a railroad. Our first prospecting trip for Henney had been a dismal failure.

Simpson's fabulous copper showing fared no better. Although he had good copper ore, subsequent exploration showed the ore to be only a small deposit not worth developing. Walker and Erickson did no better either, for their fabulous galena deposit was also too small to be of any commercial value.

Still, Henney grubstaked us for another prospecting expedition. He supplied us with a new map of the region based on an aerial survey and printed by the Government of Canada. On a scale of four miles to one inch, it showed detail we had never seen before on any map, such as every bend in the rivers, minute islands and reefs, cabins, and all known portages. It proved to be a great help to us, yet somehow such detailed information blunted the excitement of exploration. The North as I knew it lost some of its enchantment for after that when I travelled I knew what to expect before I got there, especially odd when moving through unknown territory.

Much to my surprise I found that Hanson Lake, the lake in which I had been interested for years, was now on the map. Back when I had located mining claims for Government inspection at Phantom Lake with Mr. Webster, he had told me that he was compiling a new accurate map of the region and that he would name a lake for me. This was my first knowledge that he had done so and I was amazed that he had chosen at random a lake that by coincidence was of great interest to me.

Back at our base camp on Hanson Lake we worked eastward all the way to the Sturgeon-weir River. Along the river we found a great deal of mineral and staked eight claims on an area showing iron sulphide. It had all the worthless mineralization to excite the mind of a greenhorn prospector. This time he has found a fortune. Every time we drilled and blasted and looked at the nice colours of newly-broken rock, we took out the prospector's manual. Sometimes, as we compared the text to the ore samples gathered and by studying the trench blasted out of the rock our imaginations told us that there was everything—copper, zinc, nickel, and silver—maybe even some gold! The samples looked so good that I convinced my partners that we should hurry back to Flin Flon to get everything assayed.

Our trench was sixty feet long and six feet deep when we left and began our long walk overland with our samples. We travelled east-ward for five days, prospecting as we went and carrying along with the ore samples only our food and one tarpaulin and a few mining tools. All we found were a few specks of copper. Fairburn and Vessy continued on to Flin Flon while I retraced our trail to our base camp. As it was September I asked Fairburn to pick up two or three dogs. I awaited their return at the base camp where I prospected and worked on our trench.

Fairburn and Vessy returned after nine days, leading two dogs. Our samples, alas, were only worthless mineral. Hopes were dashed again and I was beginning to realize that the life of a prospector is one of great expectations and great disappointments. The quest for a big strike followed by failure had been matched by countless other prospectors before us and future fortune hunters would experience similar ups and downs. It seemed to me at this time that one might do better just to try to find the fabled pot of gold at the end of the rainbow.

Even for those who did strike a rich vein, one that a mining company took an option on, very often the vein was never mined because the deposit turned out to be too small to be viable.

12

AT THE RAINBOW'S END

THE NEXT DAY OUR COURSE was set for Pelican Narrows. Our first camp was at Scoop Rapids once again, so we could catch fish for the dogs and for our frying pan. Two days were spent there prospecting on the east side of the river. It was the first day of October.

One day Jim Fairburn developed a sore jaw. When it became somewhat swollen and quite painful I suggested that we had better return to Flin Flon for medical attention. Just before we were going to leave we met three Indians, one of whom spoke English. When they saw that Fairburn's neck was swollen this Indian said that Fairburn must have come down with the mumps for many young boys were down with the disease at Pelican Narrows. When I asked Fairburn if he had ever had the mumps when he was young, he replied, "Not that I can recall, Olaf."

By this time we were all certain that he had the mumps. We then continued upstream and camped at Birch Portage that night. On the following day we were at Mirond Lake Portage and only about fifteen miles from Pelican Narrows. It was so windy that we had to camp there for the night. The next day it was still blowing hard from the north-west and getting quite cold. We skirted the west shore to have as much shelter as possible for our two canoes and one motor.

Fairburn's condition was steadily growing worse. We were desperate now to reach Pelican Narrows for his chest was beginning to swell. This was Friday. Every Saturday was 'plane day' at Pelican Narrows so that we could put Fairburn on the plane for Flin Flon. As it happened the plane was a day early this time for when we were only six miles from Pelican Narrows the plane came in right over us and put down behind the hills to the northward, stayed there for about half an hour and then took off in the direction of Flin Flon.

The wind velocity was increasing again as we threaded the canoes through the narrows. We could see the village at last in the distance and above the rolling whitecaps. By following close to the north shore we were able to make a landing in a small bay. The wind was blowing so hard that we could not reach the dock which made it necessary to carry our loads about three times as far to the bunkhouse as it would have been from the dock.

We had been lucky to get to Pelican Narrows that evening for the wind was increasing by the hour. It felt good to get into the bunkhouse and warm up. By now we were certain that Fairburn was not suffering from mumps, but something much more deadly was dragging him down.

He was a very sick man. I went out and asked the fur company manager when he could expect the next plane.

"Next Thursday at the earliest but likely on Friday," he said.

We were now in a very serious situation. There was no two-way radio here and the plane was not due for another week. It was too stormy to take our patient by canoe to Flin Flon where the nearest doctor was to be found.

The first thing that could be done was to apply hot poultices. Vessy and I kept up a continuous vigil, changing the poultices often and regularly. The swelling was beginning to discolour and I began fearing the worst— blood poisoning. That night was the last time he was able to swallow solid food. The first night we changed poultices every two hours, by the next night it was every hour and by the following day the swelling had risen to above his ears.

Fairburn then asked me to lance the swelling in the area of one side of his neck where the trouble had begun. I went over and asked the trading post manager what he thought about the idea of me making an incision with a razor.

He thought a moment, then said very seriously, "Don't do it. He may lose too much blood and die. Then you are apt to be charged with manslaughter or even murder. Go to the mission and ask the priest for some morphine tablets."

The priest gave me three tablets. That night Fairburn slept for the first time since we had arrived.

Vessy and I continued to change the poultices around the clock.

At noon on Monday Fairburn asked for more morphine and we gave him the second one. He slept for a time but that night we administered the third tablet. This was accomplished after a great deal of difficulty as our patient was barely able to swallow the beef broth we had been feeding him. On Tuesday he begged me to give him more morphine.

I went back to see the priest.

"It is not safe to use too much morphine," he said, but he put two more tablets into my hand, one for Tuesday and another for Wednesday. We were hoping for the plane to show up on Thursday.

We still had hopes that the swelling might open up and drain and therefore continued the poultice applications. The wind blew strongly every day until Wednesday when it eased off and then became calm. We could have left by canoe that day but poor Jim Fairburn was in no condition to travel for he was near death. It was hopeless.

By Thursday morning his head and neck were grotesquely swollen and I did not think that he could live out the day.

The plane arrived about 10:30 A.M. on Thursday. No time was lost in unloading it and making a bed in the aircraft to accommodate the patient. That was our last parting. Jim Fairburn died in the Flin Flon Hospital on the following Wednesday.

Jim Fairburn could possibly have been saved had the two-way radio installation there not been removed in 1930 as an economy measure. I asked the post manager why this had been done.

"It was run by the government. They said that it was too expensive to maintain, what with paying a salary to the operator," was his answer.

In the 1930s it seemed that no government agency was interested in saving lives of wilderness dwellers. Not only my partner, but others I knew, were not able to get out in time. Because of the lack of communication facilities, they too lost their lives. I never got over the fact that the only two-way radio had been taken away from the Pelican Narrows community after it had been installed. I always believed in progress. Any time there are a few hundred people in one place in the wilderness and there is no doctor it seems to me that the only direct link with the outside world should be the last thing to go. In later years the two-way radio came into general use where any kind of a settlement was established and proved to be a godsend to natives and whites alike.

Vessy and I sadly left Pelican Narrows for our Jan Lake camp. We had bought another dog at the trading post to give us a team of three.

Our catch in the 1935–36 trapping season was average for fox, coyote, and lynx, but our mink pelts numbered twenty-six. In March Vessy and I trekked to Flin Flon. Vessy, it seems, had been lonely without his old partner so now he went working for a man who was doing diamond drilling. He was not coming back to Jan Lake and had most of his effects with him because was hoping to get a job at the mine. Later I learned that he did not get hired on but went to England then to South Africa, where he worked in a gold mine.

The old partnership gone forever, I went back to Jan Lake. We had all parted the best of friends. As a final closing to our years of association I sold most of my traps, as well as Vessy and Fairburn's, to the Hudson's Bay Company at Pelican Narrows.

Even Revillon Frères, our supplier of long standing, had been sold to the Hudson's Bay, who had replaced the familiar sign on the old store.

I had freighted all my effects from Jan Lake to Birch Portage by dog team, leaving only the stove and some dishes in the cabin. I did not expect to return here for the purpose of trapping. I made one trip on foot from Birch Portage to Flin Flon, gathering some ore samples on the way, and had them assayed to find they were nothing but worthless rock.

In the spring of 1936 after the lakes had opened up I left by canoe for Beaver Lake. Here I found Oliver Walker, the prospector that I had met at Hanson Lake in the previous summer. He was on his way to Deschambault Lake with Angus McKenzie as his native guide. Walter asked if I would like to join him in this prospecting venture.

"I would be glad to go with you," was my reply.

In early June our party of three set out for Deschambault Lake. By now I had become well known to anyone living along the Sturgeon-weir River and any time we met someone there was always a stop to visit. We did some prospecting along the upper section of the river, then at Mirond Lake and we arrived at Deschambault Lake in due course. We made the trip to Jan Lake, where we stayed in my camp for two days. Then, at a portage between Pelican Lake and Deschambault Lake, we spent a further two days, prospecting all the while, but found nothing of interest to anyone.

We had set out for Deschambault Lake Settlement but became wind bound, which made it necessary for us to put in at an island east of the settlement. To pass the time we went prospecting. We had walked only a short distance when we found an old trench marked by two moss-covered claim posts. We returned to the canoe for a drill and the two jack-hammers then drilled two holes in the well-mineralized vein. Two dynamite charges were set off whereupon Walker announced, "I have seen a lot of iron ore bodies but I have never seen one with such a bright silver colour."

Oliver Walker had a Prospector's Handbook but the more we studied this volume, the less we seemed to know about minerals.

It certainly did look like silver. Right away we decided to stay and went to work with enthusiasm, drilling and blasting frequently. After every blast we saw bright silver-coloured ore. This ore could be cut with a knife but after about one day the silver sheen took on a bronzy appearance. Then we believed we had annabergite nickel ore.

After trenching for seven days a new form of mineralization turned up. This time we believed it was pitchblende (according to the Prospector's Handbook). Our imaginations told us that we were millionaires for sure because up to that time the only pitchblende of any consequence in the North had been found at Great Bear Lake.

The blasting could be heard from the village and soon we had daily visits from the Indians. They told us they were all going to Pelican Narrows for Treaty Day, an annual event when the Government of Canada handed out a pittance to each person under the terms of their treaty.

Our grocery supply being depleted, we accompanied the Indians to Pelican Narrows for the annual Treaty Day celebrations. Our tent was set up about a mile from the settlement where we celebrated for two days and attended all the dances. Angus McKenzie from our party was one of the fiddlers. Everyone joined in the dancing, old and young. We all had fun and were happy to be part of the celebration.

After Treaty Day we resumed prospecting and staking at Deschambault Lake, but found nothing of interest. We grew anxious to have our samples assayed, certain that our fortunes had been made, and made a fast trip to Flin Flon in three days' time. The next day Walker took all the samples over to the Hudson Bay Mining and Smelting Company office. When he got back to the hotel, I took one look at Walker and knew at once that we had drawn a blank once more.

The first words he said were, "We do not have pitchblende and the other samples will be assayed tomorrow by 4 P.M."

Next day when Walker returned from the assay office he handed me the assay sheet. All we had was iron sulphide (fool's gold) with only a trace of copper, silver and gold—and more experience.

No time was wasted on any of these claims but I made one more trip to Deschambault Lake with Walker and Angus McKenzie. I did not stay long with them after that but left for Flin Flon. Before I departed I lent Walker my big game rifle, a much-used .280 calibre Ross.

At Flin Flon I went to work for Henning on a trenching job at one of his claims with a man named Joe Zeek. One day Henning came to the site with groceries for us.

"Olaf," he said, "When I was in Flin Flon I saw Angus McKenzie with his face all bandaged up."

We were camped at Phantom Lake and not far from Flin Flon. I hurried to town to see what had happened to Angus. When I saw him I was greatly shocked at his appearance. I asked what had happened.

"A few days after you left I decided to clean your rifle and try it out on a target. As the shot went off the whole bolt blew out backwards and cut my cheek to the bone."

The doctors had set his cheek bone and patched up his face but he carried a horrible scar for the rest of his life. I have often wondered how I could have been so lucky as to miss having this happen to me, who had used that same rifle for many years.

I worked for Henney until November. After the ice became thick enough to haul freight, Sudbury Drilling Company began to drill on Henney-Mahoney mining property. I obtained work firing a steam boiler on this project. The boiler was used to heat water for the drill—a necessary procedure in winter drilling. That job lasted until April of 1936.

I moved to Beaver Lake where I had left my canoe and the one that Vessy had given me when he went away. With these two canoes I spent a month guiding sports fishermen to the good fishing spots. One Sunday I had a Mr. and Mrs. Johnson as clients. They were anxious to go to a good fishing ground for a ten to twelve day holiday.

"I know the exact place to go—Jan Lake," I told them. "I have a good cabin there and everything to make a great vacation."

A week later we were on our way. It was July so no fish were in Scoop Rapids to be scooped out, but we made our first overnight camp there anyway. On Mirond Lake on our second day out we enjoyed the scenery of summer in the North. On the third day we tied up at Pelican Narrows for a short visit and beached at the Jan Lake camp that evening just ahead of a heavy thunder storm with lots of rain. All the next day a high wind blew but it became calm that evening and we took the canoe out, started to fish and caught several jackfish and pickerel—enough to last us for two days. I believe that the Johnsons were among the first if not the very first sports fishermen ever to come to Jan Lake.

The last time I had trapped at Tulabi Lake I had left my sixteen-foot canoe (the first canoe I had ever bought rather than making myself) and a tent there. On a fine day I asked Mr. and Mrs. Johnson to take me to Tulabi Lake so I could portage my canoe and tent back to Jan Lake, and then pick me up at about 6 P.M. The Johnsons could then use this smaller canoe to travel among the islands, rocks, and shoals where they would experience the best kind of sport fishing.

As they left me out of the canoe at Tulabi Portage, I walked the three miles to the first small lake, followed its shore for a further three miles, then across a one-mile portage to Tulabi Lake to a spot where my canoe and tent had been cached more than one year previously. When I reached the canoe I found that a bear had ripped all the canvas off one side and part of the other. The canoe was otherwise intact except for a small piece of planking which had fallen off. The tent had been ripped also.

I carried everything back across the one-mile portage to the small lake. By removing all the tent ropes and tying the tent canvas tightly around the belly of the canoe I was able to paddle my way along shore in the canoe. Each time the canoe became half full of water I dragged it to shore and dumped it for I had no receptacle to use for bailing.

I did not reach the three-mile stage of this portage until 6 P.M. and I ate my lunch when I was half way across. When finally I laid down my burden on Jan Lake's shore it was 7:30 P.M. Mr. and Mrs. Johnson were waiting for me on shore with a mosquito smoke going.

To transport my canoe we placed it across the big freighter. Thus we reached the camp safely.

We freighted this canoe again on our return trip to Beaver Lake, the place of our departure. Later I re-canvassed my small canoe and sold it to the Johnsons.

Next I went to work for a man in Flin Flon who had me blast out a hole to build his new home upon. Basements in Flin Flon must be blasted rather than dug because the place is built on solid rock.

After that I met three carpenters who had been laid off at the mine. They were interested in cutting firewood and asked me if I knew of a likely location for such a venture.

"I know just the place you are looking for," I told them.

When I showed them a fire-killed jack pine stand where there were at least five hundred cords of wood, the result was a partnership of four

men including myself. Near Raymond Lake I joined in the actual cutting with axe and saw; the first time I had cut cordwood for sale since I was sixteen years old in Minnesota.

We was hauled the wood to Flin Flon on the Beaver Lake Road by truck and sold it for $1.25 a cord. Somehow I managed to average two cords a day and we stayed at this work for most of the winter.

One day we ran out of coffee and I went to the Beaver Lake Store. Here I met Eddy Darbyshire who ran a commercial fishing operation on Beaver Lake but was anxious to go to Reindeer Lake to work for Turnbull Airways. In his absence he wanted me to operate his local fishing establishment. Fishing was more in my line than cutting cordwood and I had somehow gotten over my vow never to fish for the other fellow again. The fishing lasted for seven weeks and I earned $260. Darbyshire sent word for me to put up ice for summer fishing. I earned extra money by hiring a man and renting a horse for hauling the ice and the sawdust to insulate it against thawing.

Beaver Lake was becoming civilized as more and more people were spending their holidays there. I cut and hauled ice for the Beaver Lake Hotel and also cut and skidded logs to be used in the building of log cabins.

All this time I was living at Darbyshire's. One night as I was cooking my supper there was a knock on the door and I called to my visitor to come in. I was very surprised to see Oliver Walker, the prospector, walk in the door. He told me that he had been trapping all winter, and had made a grubstake, as well as a deal with some miners to go prospecting. The miners would supply Walker with groceries and a canoe on equal shares should he find a mine—the usual agreement at that time.

I had had my fill of prospecting the summer before and I told Walker so, but I did arrange for one of the local native men to go with him.

A few days later, when Darbyshire returned from Reindeer Lake, he asked me to go into partnership with him for the summer fishing season. At this time there was a growing interest in raising mink because the pelts were bringing good prices. I thought his offer was a good one and accepted it.

After summer fishing we bought ten female and two male mink and began to build pens for them.

In the winter of 1937–38 I did the fishing while Darbyshire tended to

Olaf Hanson and his bride, Renee, on their wedding day, July, 1940.

the mink. After the fishing season we cut cordwood and sold it in town. Everyone heated with wood in those days.

In the spring of 1938 I was employed on fire patrol for the Forestry Department during the summer months. To keep my fishing job as an ace-in-the-hole, I hired a fisherman to take my place, but I made no profit on that deal for fish prices were once again very low.

During the winter of 1938–39, Darbyshire and I were fishing and cutting cordwood once again. By this time we had over forty mink and we sold a few, keeping thirty of the best animals for breeding stock. In our spare time we built more mink pens. That spring I returned to the Forestry Department to fight forest fires.

There was a continuing steady development taking place along the eastern shore of Beaver Lake. Resort cabins were going up and more people were coming there to spend their summer vacations swimming, boating, and fishing.

There I first met Miss Renee Mayrand. She had originally come from Saskatoon but was employed by the General Hospital in Flin Flon. In that summer of 1939 she was vacationing at Denare Beach for a month. As we got to know each other I found out that she loved the northland and she told me that she would like to live in this country. We planned to be married in the following summer.

Renee went back to Saskatoon for the winter while I went back to winter fishing, cutting cordwood, and increasing the size of the mink ranch.

On June 15, 1940, Renee and I were married. I went back to work for the Forestry Department. That summer Darbyshire decided to start a sawmill and go into the lumber business. He asked me to sell the mink and be his third partner but I declined his offer.

At the beginning of the Second World War, fur prices tumbled. I turned everything over to Norman's Mink Ranch on half shares and in the winter of 1940–41 continued to fish and cut cordwood—a sure way to get some cash in my pocket.

In 1941 I was back with the Forestry Department. That summer Renee and I lived in a Forestry Department cabin until the fire season ended.

In the fall of that year we went to Birch Portage to trade with the natives for their furs to a man named Shorty Russick on a percentage of the profit. This was not a lucky undertaking for me. In the beginning I traded for quite a large quantity of furs, but as I had a competitor trading there, my business fell off because of the small number of trading families in the region. My competitor and I were friends and neighbours, but

Renee and Olaf on the North
Saskatchewan River in Saskatoon,
Boxing Day, 1942.

enemies as traders. My wife thoroughly enjoyed our antics as one tried to out-do the other in fur trading. In fact, she considered living in isolation to be a wonderful experience.

After the news that Japan had bombed Pearl Harbour we somehow lost our interest in the race to get the most fur. Later that winter we received the disappointing news that the price of furs had dropped by fifty per cent of what we had paid. I realized that we must take a loss on this venture and the best of the fur season was over. When I saw Russick he confirmed that there would be no profit this season.

I decided to call all the natives together at Birch Portage. Since fur prices were too low and uncertain for trading, I asked them all to move closer to Flin Flon and cut cordwood for sale. Russick agreed that this would help us all. We moved to Johnson Lake, about twenty-two miles from Flin Flon, where I repaired an old cabin as a place for us to live while I continued trading cordwood.

The Indians worked well and cut some three hundred and fifty cords. In this way we were able to collect some of the credit extended and the people were able to make a living to see them through the winter, but there was still no profit on the entire trading operation.

My wife and I made our home here for two months. I was disappointed in the failure of the trading but Renee said it had been a great experience and that we should try trading again next year.

The natives did ask us to come back to Birch Portage and trade next winter but I knew that there was always a certain risk involved. There were outstanding accounts in this business that had a way of becoming uncollectible, and what with the instability of fur prices, I decided not to come back to trade.

Instead I returned to commercial fishing. In the winters of 1942 and again in 1943 I worked at Darbyshire's sawmill.

In the spring of 1943 I bought a house and leased a place to grow a garden at Beaver Lake. Here on the four-acre lease I grew a fine garden. In the two years that we lived there we grew and sold strawberries and also raised one hundred chickens each year. To try to help things along I did some commercial fishing but again this did not pay, with the result that I looked once more to the northern horizon.

In the fall of 1945 I went into partnership with Frank Ethier to operate a fishing camp at Reindeer Lake. At the end of August Renee and I left Beaver Lake for Flin Flon where we rented a suite. A month later I was on my way to Reindeer Lake while Renee stayed in Flin Flon. Ethier moved to another camp leaving me in charge of the first.

We were in for another bad year financially. The weather was contrary from the beginning. A few days after Reindeer Lake first froze over, two feet of snow fell so that it insulated the thin ice against further freezing. By this time long-distance freighting was being done with "cat trains" on Reindeer Lake. That winter three crawler-type tractors ("cats") went through the ice. Two drivers were lost and their bodies never recovered.

I caught a lot of fish but only half the catch got to market before the return of warm weather. Even that quantity arrived too late, for by that time the market had slipped downward. The other half of the catch was caught on the road by thawing weather in March and had to be dumped. The first half paid only the wages of the fishermen I had hired.

I went trapping that spring and made more than $500 trapping muskrats.

In November 1945 my daughter Marylin was born. I had sold my house at Beaver Lake by this time. My partner Frank Ether had stayed at Reindeer Lake to do some summer fishing to make enough money for winter supplies. I left on August 15 for Reindeer Lake where I built a new camp on Sandy Island. Today this island is the site of a landing strip for wheeled aircraft.

The winter of 1946–47 saw one of the lowest fish catches ever on Reindeer Lake. Most fishermen ended the season with a very small tonnage and only a few made any money.

Next I went to Lynn Lake to stake claims for Lew Parres. It was the time of the Lynn Lake staking rush following a new nickel-copper discovery by Sherritt Gordon Mines. After three weeks of staking I was hired by the Saskatchewan Government to locate a better route for the winter freight road southward of Reindeer Lake. The road in use at that time had two steep hills and a very poor river crossing where thin ice caused continued problems. I completed this assignment at about the end of March.

After that I resumed my work for Lew Parres staking claims near Flin Flon to be much closer to my family. At this time I worked with Roy Leslie of Wekusko, Manitoba.

On May 2, 1947 Leslie and I left by air for Lynn Lake where we prospected all summer for Parres, the work lasting until October. Then I was home in Flin Flon until mid-December when the ice was safe enough for freighting and we left for Lynn Lake. I worked as a helper on a diamond drilling outfit owned by Parres and MacMillan, a job that lasted well on into April 1948, when I returned to Flin Flon with Louie Mazo, a helper on our outfit.

Mazo had talked to me that winter and asked me to go prospecting with him in the Beaver Lake country. He told me that he had been searching the area since 1924 and in his opinion there was yet a chance of finding a rich mineral deposit. I, as usual, was ready to try anything, besides I wanted to be working close to my home and family.

We were looking for gold. By aircraft we were landed with one month's supply of groceries in an area that, said Mazo, had looked mighty interesting to him. During our stay there I made two trips to Flin Flon, once on the ice of Beaver Lake and once to bring a canoe closer to our camp. I took in samples for assay on both trips, but there was nothing to warrant staking.

Soon after I had brought in the canoe I was ready to give up and go to Flin Flon to look for employment. At the last moment I changed my mind and began to work in a very rusty outcropping, a place we had walked across almost every day as we followed a game trail over it.

When we blasted the first shot we knew that we had nickel and copper. Then we were trenching for three days, staked a few claims, and left for Flin Flon. The assay confirmed that we had mining ore!

On our return we staked more claims. As is usual in such a case, news of our find got around quickly and in a few weeks the country for miles around had all been staked.

Mazo and I optioned our claims to International Nickel for a $1000 down payment so that for once we got paid for our work. Then we went to work for the company, cutting lines for water.

Following this I went prospecting at Big Island on Beaver Lake where at first I found a copper showing. There were some old trenches which also showed copper and I found more as I searched about and improved the property. These claims were optioned two different times by two different companies. But mine was the experience of many for no drilling was done on them—the only work was the trenching I blasted to hold the claims.

Early in December of 1948 I went to work for Mid-West Drilling Company and with Mazo drilled on our original copper-nickel claims north-west of Beaver Lake. The final assays of our great find showed that it would never become a mine because the mineral content was too low. Again our hopes were shattered just as a dynamite charge shatters solid rock.

I spent some time then at line cutting but on May 1, 1949 I began work with Saskatchewan Mining and Exploration, a government agency, locating all old trenching in the Beaver Lake and Wildnest Lake regions to the eastern border of Saskatchewan.

That summer I rented a cabin at Denare Beach on Beaver Lake so that my wife and daughter could spend the summer at the resort. I remember Renee telling me how much she enjoyed living at the place where we had first met and to be able to go swimming every day.

One day in mid-July when I was away at work there occurred an incident that brought my world crashing down about me. On this day my wife and two friends went down to the beach. Renee went in for a swim and while talking to her friends from the water she suddenly sank from their sight. These ladies were non-swimmers who rushed for help at once. There were very few people about that day so that nearly twenty-five minutes elapsed before two men located her and brought her ashore. A doctor who was holidaying at the beach was hastily summoned, and did everything possible to save her, but it was too late. Subsequent examination showed that there was no water in her lungs. The cause of her sinking was uncertain, but the medical opinion was that Renee had suffered a heart attack.

13

IN ROCKBOUND COUNTRY

A FTER THE DEATH of my wife, my sister-in-law and my mother-in-law suggested to me that they look after my daughter, at that time three and one-half years old. There was nothing else I could do and I was very fortunate in that they provided the best kind of home for her.

I was with Saskatchewan Mining and Exploration until fall. After that I did some trenching on Big Island in Beaver Lake. During freeze-up it became most difficult to cross back and forth to the mainland to reach the cabin I occupied at that time. The ice had been too weak for safe crossing and I waited a few days for things to improve while colder temperatures thickened the ice a little more each day. One day as I was waiting on the main shore I received word that two men had walked across the ice to Big Island near its north end.

The following morning I prepared to walk across the ice carrying only my axe and a small packsack. When I got about half way across to the island I saw the ice, which was bare of snow, looking suspiciously thin and unsafe. Many years of experience in travelling over ice had put me on the alert. I decided then that I should test the ice for thickness by cutting a small hole with my axe. The first stroke of the axe blade cut right through the ice, which cracked and immediately collapsed where I stood.

I went down almost over my head but managed to grab the edge of the ice on the side from which I had approached this death-trap.

The ice on this side was thicker than on the other, a fact which no doubt saved my life. The thick ice was therefore more stable so I clung to it for a few seconds that seemed an eternity.

Luckily I had held on to the axe as I had crashed through. I slid myself carefully upward and got myself partly out of the water onto the ice shelf. I reached out as far as I could with the axe and carefully chopped a small hole in the ice. The Hudson's Bay axe that I carried had a unique head shape, with the bottom of the outer edge of the blade tapering inward to form what can be used sometimes as a hook. Using my axe head, I hooked and dragged myself forward and away from danger. I rolled myself over and over until I lay about thirty feet away from the hole, all the while hanging on to the axe. Then I arose and began to run in the direction from which I had come.

It was two miles back to the cabin and we were in winter temperatures. To keep from freezing to death I had to run all the way back. My clothing of course became frozen stiff but this created a sealing effect, which helped contain my body's heat to some extent so that I did not suffer frostbite. When I was in the shelter of my cabin I had a most difficult time taking off my parka, which felt like armour plate. When I had stoked up the stove and changed into dry clothes I sat there soaking up the heat while my outdoor clothing thawed and dripped from the nails in the wall.

I took the time to think matters over. During my years in the wilderness, I had broken through lake ice twice before but each time I had been cautious enough to carry two long poles with me. I was then able to use the poles for support when I went through, so I only went in up to my knees and had got out without trouble. On this third occasion I had been so stupid as to neglect cutting the poles. It was a good lesson for me, seeing that I was still alive to learn from it.

A few days afterwards I went to the office of Mid-West Diamond Drilling where I asked for a job as a driller's helper. They wanted to give me a job as a runner but I did not have enough know-how, I thought, to be a runner or deep driller. I worked as a helper at Beaver Lake until one of the runners got hurt and I had to take his place. That was the last time I ever worked as a helper but every winter after that I was employed as a runner by Mid-West while each summer I prospected and did part-time diamond drilling.

Near spring break-up in 1950 I met a trapper who had fallen ill and was unable to trap. He asked me to trap for him on his trapping lease at

Copper Lake, Manitoba. I accepted his offer for one-half of the fur catch. I did the trapping, and prospected at the same time. I came up with a mining claim that was later optioned with the result that my earnings were very good for that season.

After trapping I returned to Beaver Lake and went diamond drilling for Noranda Mining on some of our claims there. Until Christmas I was with Mid-West and then I drilled for Dan MacMillan, drilling contractor.

In April, 1951, MacMillan sent me to do diamond drilling at Lyonial Lake, east of Lac La Ronge. Drill, equipment, and supplies were brought in by plane. The job was completed on June 10 when a man named Hagan, one of the crew, and I left Lyonial Lake by canoe and small outboard motor and enough gasoline and groceries to last us for ten days. We portaged from lake to lake, then followed a small river to where it joined the Churchill River west of Kettle Falls. We followed the Churchill and after portaging across Frog Portage into Wood Lake we had good travelling down the lakes and into the familiar Sturgeon-weir to Beaver Lake. The whole trip had been made in six days, including one day when we had to sit out a rainstorm.

Back once more in Flin Flon I met a drilling contractor from near Birch Lake, a place about two miles east of Beaver Lake near the Manitoba border. I worked with him until August when the contract for the main road to Flin Flon was completed. After that I was prospecting for a month, then diamond drilling for Noranda Mining and Exploration until freeze-up when I continued my regular winter job with Mid-West until April 1952.

On May 20 I was on my way prospecting for wages and interest on any future mine for a mining exploration outfit. I travelled by canoe and motor, prospecting along the Sturgeon-weir River, Mirond Lake, Pelican Lake, Deschambault Lake, Ballantyne Bay, and then up the Oskikebuk River and back to Beaver Lake. This was more like a vacation for me over familiar trails and new country alike, and I even had a sponsor nowadays. There were only memories of past struggles for survival, and these memories were gradually fading....

On this journey I had staked a group of claims on the Southeast Arm of Deschambault Lake.

Now I prospected on the west side of Missi Island on Beaver Lake, where I found copper ore of some interest. A group of claims was staked there in partnership with a friend who had two mining discoveries to his credit. On these particular claims we have done a good deal of trenching over the years in order to hold them and they had been optioned to mining companies on three different occasions. At this writing, no drilling has ever been done on these copper showings.

In the same year as we had staked these claims we also did some trenching and some line cutting until it was time to get off the lakes because of the coming freeze-up. After that I was with Mid-West until the spring break up of 1953.

That summer I went prospecting for my old boss Lew Parres on a wage and interest agreement. Then it was back to Missi Island to do some more trenching on our copper claims. When we optioned them the first time we were in great hopes that we had struck it rich but after a time they sent our claims back and there was no diamond drilling done there. We continued with the trenching and began to look for another mining company that might be interested.

In the latter part of October, just before winter set in, I went to Elbow Lake, Manitoba to prospect and stake claims for Parres, and arrived back in Flin Flon in early December.

After the Christmas holidays I returned once again to Hanson Lake. I had a native helper and we staked some claims at a place where I had found a light-assay copper showing, for Parres on interest. These claims were later optioned to a mining company who drilled several holes on the property but then left for good.

In the spring of 1954 I was drilling for Parres and that summer I prospected and staked for him again. That fall I was back with Mid-West working at my regular winter job as a deep driller.

14

REINDEER LAKE TO LYNN LAKE

O NE NIGHT AS I returned to my room in Flin Flon after work I found a note. In my absence a telephone call had come in for me from the Saskatchewan Department of Natural Resources. I was to call their office in Prince Albert. I had no idea of the reason but when I had finished my evening meal I contacted them.

My caller advised me that he had recently returned from Reindeer Lake, where the local commercial fishermen had asked him to hire me to locate an all-weather road from Kinoosao on Reindeer Lake eastward to the new mine at Lynn Lake so that a link could be established with the railroad being built northward from Sherridon, Manitoba. Kinoosao, which at that time was called Co-op Point, was the centre of the commercial fishing industry at Reindeer Lake.

At once I began to think of the difficulty that one can encounter while travelling in this country at the onset of winter so I mentioned to my caller that this was not the best time of the year to locate a road.

"We want to start bulldozing this road as early as possible so that it can be used later this winter," was his reply.

I asked him why they had chosen me for the job.

"You are the only man we know who can do the locating. You have the experience," he explained.

At any other time of the year I would have been willing to take on such work; also, since I was employed, I would have to give notice to my employer. In the end I promised to do work at the same wages I was earning with my present employer plus expenses.

The company found a man to take my place during my absence. They were very good about it, assuring me that because they needed roads in the North I would be granted a leave of absence and my job would be waiting for me on my return.

The next day I again called Natural Resources in Prince Albert, pointing out that at this time of year the only way that we could move our camp and our supplies was to pack everything on our backs, as no aircraft could land when the ice was forming on the lakes. In short, it was essential that I have a helper. They asked me if I knew of anyone locally who might prove satisfactory for this work. I would have to look for one. Then the suggestion was made that they send out a chap from Prince Albert, to which I agreed. This would save valuable time in getting the outfit together and we would be ready to leave in two days.

It was the morning of October 14 that my man Frank Timpson showed up at the Flin Flon Hotel. I was happy to get someone with experience in locating roads. Timpson said he had left Prince Albert in such a hurry that he had little chance to pick up any maps of the country where we were to work, except one drawn to the scale of twenty miles to an inch, which showed very little detail. This was unsuitable so I looked up a geologist in Flin Flon who supplied us with maps in much greater detail.

At 9 A.M. on October 15 Timpson and I left Flin Flon by plane with Parson's Airways. At Lynn Lake I purchased an aluminium canoe, tent, stove, cooking equipment, and sleeping bags. Our groceries were to be picked up at Co-op Point on Reindeer Lake. The whole outfit was so organized that it would be ready to move on very short notice.

I had the pilot fly over the country where we were to locate the new road. It was a nice sunny day and from the air the terrain looked fairly good. I was glad to see that all the larger lakes were still free of ice so that we could make a landing. Then I had the pilot circle back to a lake about thirty miles east of Co-op Point. This was McMillan Lake, where I had decided to set up our first camping place and begin to work westward to our destination of Co-op Point.

During the first three days we blazed our way too far south and were stopped at a muskeg where we could push a pole down about twelve feet before it touched the bottom. This was no crossing for a summer road so it was necessary to find a better place. I had seen this muskeg as we had flown over it and knew that it was several miles long but would have to be crossed somewhere. About a mile north of our first crossing attempt we found a place that was only three or four feet down to solid ground, near a good growth of tamarack large enough to cut down and use to lay a corduroy road. In the centre of the crossing was a small creek with very little current, which could be very easily bridged and the approaches filled in without any problem.

After this we made good progress with our blazing. We had taken enough food for three days but our supplies had all but run out. We marked a big tree and struck out for Co-op Point, planning to blaze back to this spot on our return.

We had almost reached Co-op Point by the time darkness fell, but we could not get across a small bay to the store and had to camp overnight while listening to the dogs howling and someone chopping wood over in the village. The last of our supplies was consumed that night and we were thankful that we were warm in our robes and only a half-mile from the store.

Our breakfast next morning was coffee—all we had left. In the daylight we found a trail to the store quickly, and arrived in about an hour by going around the bay. The store manager served us a proper breakfast, and said there would be a plane coming next morning, the last one of the float season.

We had stroke of good fortune next day when the plane not only arrived but was to deliver our supplies to our base camp at McMillan Lake, enough, we estimated, to finish our entire road locating assignment. Taking the plane to our base, we unloaded everything, put it under cover, then flew back to Co-op Point. That night we bunked in a cabin with the owner Alf Olson, an old time Northerner. Next morning we began the work of locating and blazing back to the point where we had cut our last blaze, marking our way to McMillan Lake.

It was November 5 as we packed up our sleeping bags and groceries to last for four days and struck out through the bush. There was less than half an inch of snow and above zero temperatures; certainly this was going to be a late freeze-up. That day was very bright and sunny and that night in camp was warm and pleasant, in fact, very mild for November.

The second day out was mild but cloudy and after working since dawn we made camp early. The sky was overcast with low-ceilinged clouds, which meant that snow was coming, so we made a good shelter of spruce boughs. There was two inches of new snow on our bedrolls next morning, but the snowfall had stopped. It was slow slogging now, moving through the bush and blazing spruce and jack pine trees, which are the best of snow-carriers. Every tree we blazed released a cascade of snow on our heads and shoulders because it was too warm to wear our parka hoods up. It is a peculiar fact that snow falling from trees in mild weather most often lands on the back of your bare neck.

After the noon lunch the sun was out and by 4 P.M. the snow had almost all melted from the trees. Our clothing was soaking wet when we made camp that night.

Progress was slow on the third day and another camp had to be made under the stars. Much time had been spent in locating all that day so that blazing had not progressed either. Our food had to be rationed at this time for there remained only a bit of bacon, some butter, half a loaf of bread, and some coffee. There was no need to worry for we were confident that we would arrive at our base at McMillan Lake sometime on the following day. We hung our soggy clothing by the campfire again and by 9 P.M. it was nicely dried and we were ready to roll into our robes for the night.

The morning was colder. After a necessarily light breakfast we got back to work. Due to the time lost in locating the best route for this marker to the blazed line, we did not reach our planned noon stop until almost dark.

Happy to have found the line at last, we ate our lunch of half a sandwich each. It was eight miles to the tent, clear and moonlit, the blazes easily visible as they led us to the tent by midnight.

Our groceries were found to be in good order as was everything else we had left there. No time was lost in preparing a good meal as a reward for another hard journey of packing sleeping robes, cooking equipment, axes, and dwindling groceries.

When we turned in I believe that Frank Timpson fell asleep at once. It was not long before I was dead to the world also, but before I slept I recall thinking that it was three weeks now since we had started working together, three weeks of hard going, yet I had heard not one word of complaint from him. I thought of all the men with whom I had travelled in the past and I could not recall any one of them who did not, sooner or later, find something to complain about; but not Frank Timpson.

The next day we rose late and did not resume work until noon. Working eastward, we located about four miles of roadway. McMillan Lake was at last beginning to freeze over so we hurriedly loaded everything into the canoe and paddled across the lake to the east shore. Then we portaged everything over to a small lake but the ice on this lake was too thin for safe crossing so we set up our tent on its shore. Two days we spent locating and blazing, by which time the ice on the small lake was stronger and safe enough for travel. Frank and I re-loaded the canoe and pulled it across, one man pulling and the other balancing the canoe on its keel, which then served as a sleigh runner.

In this region it was slow going for as we worked on the road we had to take time out to portage our outfit overland in relays to keep it in reasonable distance from our work. Camp was moved at about five mile intervals.

The best road location at this time led us to the north shore of another lake where, in mild weather once more, we decided to move our camp to the east shoreline by the canoe skidding method. As we were about half way across, the ice began to crack under our feet. In the event we should break through we planned to board the canoe. In preparation we had cut two poles that we could use to break our way to better ice or to shore if necessary. In this case the canoe did not break through but we walked on the poles and our paddles as we moved the canoe, one man on each side, and thus eventually to shore and to safety. Farther to the south we could see this same lake was free of ice.

It was a very mild night. The wind, blowing from the south, had buffeted us as we moved slowly on our way across the very thin ice. It was dark and cloudy and at 8 P.M. we had reached the far shore.

We got out our candle lanterns, which are made from a four pound jam or syrup tin, and shine a beam of light the way a flashlight does. Just cut a hole in the side of a can fairly close to the bottom. The hole should be slightly smaller than the diameter of the candle. Leave the edge rough to hold the candle when it is inserted from the inside of the can. Make a wire handle by punching two nail holes, one at the bottom rim and one at the top rim so that you can insert and secure a wire. With such a light I have walked miles in the dark on lakes while facing the wind and very rarely did the wind ever blow out my candle. The bottom of the can keeps the wind from blowing in and the inside of a new can reflects a very good light.

This was our light source that night as we put up our tent in the dark, gathered fuel, and cut boughs for our "spruce feather beds."

I went down to the shore, chopped a hole in ice two inches thick, and dipped a pail of water to boil for our tea. However in the morning when I went back for water to make coffee there was no water hole, neither was there any ice in the lake, for a thirty-mile-an-hour gale had piled it all along the shore while we slept!

This was a new experience both for Timpson and myself. Never before had we pulled a loaded canoe over the ice at night and seen open water and rolling white caps where our trail had been the night before.

The mild weather lasted only that day. In the afternoon it turned so cold that the lake froze over completely before we moved camp. Three days later we could walk safely anywhere on the lake ice.

Good luck, it seemed, was on our side as the weather turned mild again and with only two inches of snow on the ground it all made for good walking and packing our outfit. Our camp by this time was near Vanderkerckhove Lake. When it was time to move again, the packing was overland and across many small lakes on the way until we reached a creek that was still open here and there. We had to pack and skid the outfit here also but after several days we set up our camp at the northeast bay of Vanderkerckhove Lake.

There was up to five inches of ice with no snow on the ice at all. Luckily there was a good area of high level land where we were marking out the proposed road and therefore we made good progress. Two days later we encountered a river flowing out of Vanderkerckhove Lake into Goldsand Lake. We had the good fortune to find a very good crossing where the river was only fourteen feet wide. Then we were on an esker, a high gravel ridge, running generally north and south. Lynn Lake, our final destination, lay southward and to the east. This esker seemed to have been made for us and our progress was very good indeed.

Again our grocery supplies would soon have to be replenished, and we planned to walk to Lynn Lake for that purpose. One evening as we returned to the tent after work we were greeted by a visitor. He turned out to be a trapper from Brochet far to the north near Reindeer Lake's north end. He spoke English well and said that he was travelling to Lynn Lake with his three husky dogs and toboggan to sell his furs. He stayed with us that night and we decided to accompany him to town.

Our visitor said it was thirty miles to Lynn Lake. It was the end of November and the ice on the lakes was seven inches thick, and strong enough for a light plane to land, when we set out. Good time was made as we followed the dogs to Zed Lake for lunch and to Lynn Lake by 6 P.M.

We located the hotel first where we asked for a room. The hotel keeper replied that they were all filled up, and in fact there were as many as four to a room.

At that time the hotel had only eight rooms and no lobby where a man could sit down. For this luxury one would have to go to the one café in the town or to the beer parlour. Without wasting more time we went to the beer parlour for a bottle of beer apiece, then to the café for a steak after our thirty mile hike. We sat there on stools, taking our time at eating for we knew that as soon as we left the café we might have to stand on our feet all night.

Wondering where we might find a room we called in at the detachment office of the Royal Canadian Mounted Police. The constable in charge explained that since the railroad had just been completed into Lynn Lake from Sherridon, everything was filled up with railroad employees, salesmen, opportunists, and so on and he knew of no vacant accommodation anywhere. However, there were at present two empty cells downstairs where we could sleep as a last resort if we called back at midnight and they had not picked up any tenants in the meantime. It was 9 P.M. The constable directed us over to the movie theatre where we could kill the time until midnight.

After the movie and back in the beer parlour I had suggested to Timpson that there might be someone there that I knew. Sure enough, after ordering some beer and looking around at the customers I saw three men that I knew, all sitting around a table. As soon as I had finished my beer I lost no more time, but made a beeline for the one fellow I thought might have a solution for our problem that night. His name was Andy and he was a carpenter at the mine.

He looked at me in surprise and said, "Are you staking claims in this part of the country?"

"I am locating a road from Lynn Lake to Reindeer Lake," I explained. "Right now I need to find a place to sleep."

"I have a bunk at the Company bunkhouse. Neither one of us is that big that we can't bunk together."

"That will do for me, Andy," I said, "but I have a partner. I know a single bunk is thirty inches wide and pretty narrow for two men."

Andy stood up then and walked over to where Frank was sitting, swallowing the last of his beer. I made the introductions and then Andy led us to the mining company's bunkhouse while saying something about seeing what could be done for us. He looked up the caretaker and asked if there were any bunks not in use. The caretaker said that Frank could use one bunk that had been empty for three nights due to the absence of a mine worker. Then he found another bunk for me. Happily no one came in to claim either bunk that night. We used the company's shower bath and had a very fine sleep.

Our trapper friend had looked up some friend in town where he had spent the night. We met him on the street next day and found that there were no fur buyers in Lynn Lake because the only store was operated by the mining company.

The next afternoon Timpson and I were very surprised to receive an invitation from the mine superintendent to visit him at his office. When we arrived there it turned out that we had become the golden-haired boys if not minor heroes. The superintendent and all the staff were interested in what we were doing and particularly if the new road we were locating would run close to Zed Lake. With its fine sandy beaches and good trout fishing, Zed Lake would make a good summer resort for mine workers. I assured them that the road would actually follow close to the east shore of Zed Lake for a few miles.

At this office we were further surprised that the news that we had looked all over town for a bed had preceded us.

The mine superintendent said that had we contacted his office our wants would have been met at once.

He told us, "If you are ever in the same predicament in this town, please let us know. You will certainly not be left to sleep in the street if we are aware of it here."

"How are you planning to return to your camp?" he asked.

"We are looking for a small plane to take us back," I began.

"How thick is the ice?" he asked.

When I assured him that it was quite safe for a light plane he said that there were no light planes in Lynn Lake at that time but we would be flown back in the company's Beaver aircraft with their compliments.

That night the hotel sent word that they had a room for us.

Our stay in Lynn Lake ended after two days. Our grocery supply had been secured and the mining company gave us new aerial maps of the Zed Lake area that saved us a good deal of work and unnecessary locating.

It was early December and the days, of course, were very short at this northern latitude. The Beaver aircraft landed us at our camp at 11 A.M., a free ride that we very much appreciated.

About two inches of snow had fallen in our absence. At about 1 P.M. we went out to do some locating and made enough progress that we decided to move our camp about three miles southward down the lake to a good site on the eastern shore. The aluminium canoe was again used as a sled but now it was hard going, for we had to pull over scattered snowdrifts on the lake surface and the entire outfit was in the canoe. In spite of these obstacles we reached our destination by sundown, erected the tent, and cut a good supply of wood before dark.

In the morning we took our noon lunch in our packsacks and went east to an area of high hills, then walked north until we came upon our blazed line. There was good locating for us and we blazed the road from there to well south of our newest camp.

On the following day our route led us to a small lake. Then we went back all the way to Vanderkerckhove Lake via two more small lakes and then to our tent. Another day saw us moving camp again over small lakes and packing everything through thick bush. Zed Lake was getting closer. We set up camp near the road location and in two days we had blazed the line to Zed Lake—only fifteen miles from Lynn Lake.

It was only a few days before Christmas and Zed Lake would be our last camp move. Our plan was to keep on locating from here until we reached Lynn Lake. On December 20, we were beyond Little Brightsand Lake.

That night I said to Timpson, "We will leave in the morning for Lynn Lake, blazing for a while and then walk to town."

There were four inches of snow on the ground here and fair walking. That day it snowed until noon. We stopped blazing at about 2 P.M. and walked on. The last three miles to Lynn Lake were covered in darkness.

This time there was a room waiting for us in the hotel. While our 7 P.M. dinner was being served, in walked a man whom I had met long ago in my Game Guardian days. He was Frank Pakally from Livelong, Saskatchewan. Pakally told us he had shipped up crawler-type tractors and sleighs to haul fish from Reindeer Lake to Lynn Lake and was prepared to bulldoze the road we had just blazed.

Pakally next day took a Bombardier snow vehicle out to bring in our outfit from Zed Lake, but we had to contend with a great crack in the ice which ran from one shore to the other so that only part of the load could be brought in at that time. The canoe and the stove were left for the bulldozers to bring back later and shipped by rail to Flin Flon.

Frank Timpson was hired to go back to Reindeer Lake with the bulldozing outfit. I left for Flin Flon by plane on December 23, just in time for Christmas. It was nice to be back with another job finished.

While we had been locating I had not known where the road would actually be built because the road was in Manitoba even though it had been located for the Provincial Government of Saskatchewan. I am told that it is today an all-weather road with a gravelled surface. I have not been back to see this road but I certainly had a good look at the area it passes through, so as to avoid rocky hills and floating bogs.

It had taken the two of us two months and eight days to mark out this road. In summer, our party could have done it in thirty days for then there are many more hours of daylight and we could have had our camp moved by aircraft. The season chosen for us was the very worst. We had been human pack horses as we carried and pulled our outfit from one place to another. I know that Timpson and I left a few pounds of our weight on that trail between Reindeer Lake and Lynn Lake.

When I think back I wonder how many men would take on such a job today. The two of us had located and blazed about seventy miles of road through stark wilderness with no two-way radio (or any other kind of radio), very little aircraft support or outside communication, and during the freeze-up season. We were a long way behind the times.

Good luck had been with us all the way. Not one day was lost through sickness or accident. It had been a good experience, the kind that is not available any more. Graduate engineers with technology such as helicopters do this type of work today.

15

LADY PROSPECTOR

AFTER CHRISTMAS I took a trip to Prince Albert and then on to Saskatoon to visit my daughter, as I did at every opportunity. On my return to Flin Flon I went back to diamond drilling for Mid-West until July. Later that year I worked on some claims in which I had an interest.

At about the end of September I met a lady prospector who was looking for someone whom she could hire to do some drilling on her claims at Jackfish Lake in the Red Lake country of northern Manitoba, where she had a mineral deposit of nickel and copper. I owned an Exray diamond drill that could go to a depth of about 250 feet.

I agreed to drill for her if she paid all my expenses and gave me an interest in any future mine that might be developed on the property. It was October 1 before we began drilling on site. I had a helper, a chap from Wekusko, Manitoba, on the Hudson Bay Railroad.

I was almost finished the job when my diamond drill broke down. We had to canoe back to Flin Flon by way of Wekusko Lake.

We had to wait two days in Flin Flon for the drill repairs to be shipped out from Winnipeg. As it was getting late in the season I telephoned my employer to ask if she would get the groceries so we could pick them up on our return. She then instructed me to get what groceries I would need. Then she wanted to know if I could get along without a helper, an economy measure, if she came along to assist instead. I replied that I thought I could manage.

It was October 27 and the lakes could freeze over any day. I ordered enough groceries to last the two of us for about a month in the event that we should get ice-bound at the job's end.

I returned to the drill site by plane. After letting me off the pilot headed for Wekusko Lake to pick up my employer. When she arrived she was astonished that I had brought such a large stock of groceries for the estimated three days of drilling. I told her that I was not about to take any chances on our being frozen in and then have to trek out to civilization without food. I explained that if we did get out in four days I would buy back the unused groceries, and the matter was settled.

On October 30 it became very cold with no wind at all and Jackfish Lake froze over. The next day we completed the drilling but the weather was bitterly cold with a strong north wind and driving snow. A patch of ice broke up out in the middle of the lake but a float plane could not have lit there, nor could we have walked on the ice to get to it.

To make certain that no plane could come in we walked a two mile portage to Reed Lake from Jackfish Lake, carrying the lady's luggage. But Reed Lake, when we got there, was a sheet of snow-covered ice all the way across.

That was when I gave her the bad news, "We can forget about getting out of here by plane."

I was very surprised, I must say, when she replied, "I have never seen the weather so cold and wintry at this time of year."

"Lady," I said, "I have been in the North for over thirty years and have not seen any year when the lakes did not freeze up. But I always made certain that I was prepared for it. We are prepared for it now and we are not going to starve."

I learned later that her husband and son became very worried at this time. They hired two woodsmen to pack in food for us across country, who found themselves in country of so much unfrozen bog and unsafe ice that they turned back. Next her husband tried to get a plane to drop us some food parcels to keep us alive, but as it is too dangerous to fly at this season in the North, no pilot would risk even taking off, the thin ice being unsuitable for either floats or skis. Our would-be rescuers had no idea that we were well stocked with food.

The lady and I returned to our drilling site. There I found two boards, left there when someone had repaired the old caboose at the site. From

Hanson's Exray diamond drill, which could reach down to 150 feet, was in great demand in the Flin Flon area.

these boards I built a small sleigh and fashioned two sleigh runners. We stayed in camp for two days, waiting for the ice to thicken up enough for safe travel.

When the ice would carry us, we set out pulling the sleigh loaded with our sleeping robes and supplies and some equipment for camping out. First we descended Jackfish Creek where the ice was good, arriving at Reed Lake in about two hours. Our course was very close to the shoreline along which we travelled for three miles until it was time to stop for lunch.

It was a long hike to Reed Lake's outlet at the Grass River. We made good progress however and when darkness overtook us we were only three miles from Grass River. Luckily the weather was fine and not very cold. We camped on the shore that night in a stand of dry wood for our fire, where I built a good shelter of spruce poles and boughs, and put down a thick mattress of boughs for our sleeping robes.

On the second day our journey led us down the Grass River where the ice was most insecure, with open water to be seen from time to time. At one open section we portaged everything for at least five hundred yards. In other places we walked the bank, one pulling the sleigh while the other pushed with a long pole, to keep the sleigh on the ice and away from the bank. Two miles of such travelling brought us to rapids and more open water. We pulled the sleigh around the rapids at this portage but carried across most of the load.

We had our lunch at 1 P.M. I can say that this lady was an excellent camp cook and certainly very experienced in outdoor cooking. My job was to get the wood and find spruce boughs to stand upon so that our feet were out of the snow as we stood by the campfire.

The portage completed by 3 P.M. we were once again on good ice for a distance of two miles until we had to make another shorter portage. Then it was good travelling again for one more mile to the last portage. We completed the task of pulling everything across this portage of about four hundred yards just as darkness closed in.

I knew that it was only a mile to a trapper's cabin at Tramping Lake. I was ready to make camp but was surprised to hear the lady say that she was game to continue on to the cabin. She certainly could stand up to hardship.

For the present we had a cold lunch and a drink of Grass River water, then set out on our last mile for that day. It was very dark when we got to the cabin. We had expected to find someone living there but it was vacant. Inside there was an airtight heater and enough wood had been cut to start a fire and get warmed up. Wherever I travelled in the North, I always carried a supply of candles. I lit three of them now to give ample light to prepare our much-needed supper. We were both very hungry after pulling our sleigh and portaging from 8 A.M. to 8 P.M.

I picked up a tin pail and told her I was going to get some water from Tramping Lake, the shore of which was only a hundred yards from the cabin. In the dark I took my axe and walked down the trail to cut a hole in the ice to dip out water. I was in for a surprise when I got there for there was no ice. Tramping Lake was wide open!

So here we were, at the end of our travel on the ice and of course we had no canoe. We were situated about twenty miles from the Snow Lake Highway, which farther on joins the road that leads to Wekusko, our destination.

When I brought in the water I told her that there was no ice on the lake. I explained that Tramping Lake is very deep and that deep lakes freeze over later than do shallow ones, even if the shallow ones are larger in size. It was November 5 and she had an appointment in Winnipeg on November 11 to meet with mine shareholders of her Jackfish Lake claims.

On November 6 we were back to freezing temperatures. New ice was forming along the lake shore as we waited for enough thickness to allow us to travel with the sleigh. On November 7 we set out.

The ice carried the sleigh for some distance but soon we had to pass weak ice by taking to the shore. The travelling was so slow and strenuous that it took us six hours to travel three and one-half miles. Finally, our course led us to a vacant tourist cabin. This winterized structure was used for hunting in the fall and for fishing during the summer.

From the shore at the widest part of Tramping Lake no ice was to be seen anywhere. To add to our woes the weather had turned milder. This prompted me to decide to leave my client in the cabin while I walked across country to reach the Snow Lake Highway by about noon the next day.

It was November 8. I kept walking northward from Tramping Lake until dark. It had snowed heavily that afternoon. As the snow melted I got quite wet. I began to look for big spruce trees for shelter and a place to make a fire. It was a very calm evening, the kind when sounds can be heard for long distances in the wilderness. As I stood there in the dark, I heard a diamond drill working, seemingly not far away.

I decided to walk straight toward the sound of the drill. Now I was travelling westward, straight away from Tramping Lake and the highway. I do not recall how many hills I climbed nor how many bogs I crossed when I got down between the hills. Down in the muskegs I lost the sound of the drill but when I reached the top of the next hill the sound seemed to come from very close by. Walking down such steep, rocky hills is very slow going on a dark night. I used a pole about ten feet long to feel my way and to avoid falling over the precipices. I carried that pole all the way. On one muddy creek, I broke through the ice but with the pole I managed to work my way out without sinking into the morass below. I felt that I had an obligation to get help for the lady and kept going.

I arrived at the drillers' shack at midnight. I was wet all through. My parka was as soaked as if I had just pulled it out of the lake. The drilling outfit belonged to my old employers, Mid-West Drilling, but I had never seen any of this crew before. When they answered my knock on the door, I walked in looking like a wet rat. I believe they were too shocked to say anything for a minute. I asked if I could stay awhile and warm up and dry out my clothes.

One chap asked, "Are you lost?"

"No," I said quietly, "I'm not lost."

"Where did you come from?" he asked next.

"Jackfish Lake," I explained. "Do any of you know where Jackfish Lake is?"

"No, we sure don't, never heard of it," said my interrogator.

I said my hike for that day had been from near the west end of Tramping Lake.

They were preparing their midnight meal and asked me to eat with them. The main course was bacon and eggs and they indicated that they had extra food cooked. I said I had my lunch with me, but when I opened my lunch bag my sandwiches looked like they had just been fished out of a garbage can. After the smells of bacon and eggs my poor sandwiches did not appear very appetizing. I threw them out for the whiskey jacks (Canada Jays) to eat in the morning. That plate of bacon and eggs was about the best feed I can remember.

It was 4 A.M. before I got my clothes reasonably dry except for my parka, which seemed as if it would never dry out. The drillers' camp was about a mile from the drill site. They told me that I would find a spare bed there in the first tent. I stayed there that night. In the morning, the foreman stuck his head in the tent and wanted to know if I would have breakfast with the men or sleep until noon. I got up and had breakfast. I knew the cook, the foreman, and the two drillers who alternated shifts with the first two whom I had met at the drill site. This part of the crew all wanted to know how I got to the camp after midnight as there was no road to the camp, only what we called "plain service," which means walking over unmarked ground.

There was a foot path to the next drill site at a lake four miles distant. After breakfast, I walked to this site just in time for their coffee break. Now, I had six miles left to Anderson Lake and another drill site. It was 1 P.M. before I arrived there but I was in luck as I knew the foreman who told the cook to make me a lunch. I knew most of the crew as well who all asked how I got to the country at this time of year.

Now, I was five miles from Snow Lake Mine and only one mile from the highway. During the telling of my trip to all I had met, I was getting delayed in arriving at my destination, Wekusko Lake. That afternoon I got to a store on the highway situated about three miles from Snow Lake. I was well acquainted with the store owner, who was very surprised to see me on foot. After we had a cup of coffee together, this man took me to Wekusko Lake in his truck and then to the summer resort of Tramping Lake Portage, where the river coming out of Tramping Lake was wide open.

Here I rented a canoe and outboard motor. I was hoping to get back to the lady where I had left her. There was about one hour of daylight left. It was seventeen miles to where I was going, but as I ascended the river and it got wider it was frozen over. Now breaking ice with a canoe is very hard on the canvas which convinced me to give up for that day and return to Tramping Lake Portage for the night.

That night at the Portage I stayed with Mr. Marshall, who was in charge of canoes and cabins. To pass the time, I was looking at some maps of that part of the country when I found I could get to the wide part of Tramping Lake by crossing four small lakes which by now were frozen hard enough for walking safely and only one half-mile portage to contend with. It had turned cold since I left Tramping Lake.

Mr. Marshall told me that every morning the lady's husband had called in to see if anyone was prepared to fly and take him in search of his wife. About 8:30 next morning we saw him coming driving his truck. We went out and stopped him. When he saw me he seemed very surprised.

His first words were, "Where is my wife?"

"She is only seventeen miles from where we are standing," I said.

He was all smiles and was very relieved for his worries were over. I told him that I could get her out the next day and explained that I planned to cross the four lakes by pulling a small canoe over the four small lakes to open water on Tramping Lake. I would need someone to accompany me to assist with pulling the canoe.

"There is a man at my place who will go with you," he said.

With that we got into his truck and drove to his place. Here, after lunch, we picked up a light aluminium canoe and the man to help me pull it.

We pulled the canoe easily over the four lakes over good safe ice. By 3:30 that afternoon, we looked out from the shore of Tramping Lake over open water to see the tourist camp across the bay. When we had paddled across, the lady was certainly glad to see us. We did not stop for lunch as we wanted to get back to the portage before dark and to be off the lake before new ice formed that night.

We ate our lunch as it was getting dark at the portage: bacon, biscuits baked by the lady, and coffee made at the campfire. Off again on our way, all baggage in the canoe, we hauled the load over the portage. It took the three of us to haul it across the ground where the snow was only two inches deep. On the lake it was different—we made fast time, the two men in front pulling and the lady pushing from behind. We were at the highway by midnight. The lady's husband was waiting for us there beside a good campfire.

At the lady's home by about 1 A.M., we were all happy to be back. It was November 11, the day she was to have been in Winnipeg. She had to send a telegram next day from Wekusko to her mine shareholders postponing the meeting.

That night her daughter-in-law made us a wonderful home-cooked meal. We had a great celebration.

I stayed over one day, then took the train back to Flin Flon. This story has a happy ending for the claims on which we drilled were later optioned to a mining company for several thousand dollars, a fitting reward for a lady who had the drive and daring to go prospecting on her own and to arrange for and supervise the drilling.

16

THE HANSON LAKE ROAD

BACK AT FLIN FLON I went diamond drilling for Mid-West as usual until Christmas time. Then I went prospecting until the spring breakup of 1955. The balance of the year was completed with alternate stints at prospecting and drilling.

In the winter of 1955–56 I was once more employed as a diamond driller with Mid-West but that year they sent me to one of their operations in northern Manitoba. Here I met Barry Richards, the mining engineer and geologist in charge of drilling. We became well acquainted and had many talks about the North.

One evening Richards asked me if I was familiar with the country to the west and north of Flin Flon. We both noted the lack of roads in this area and the difficulties this posed for mining, commercial fishing, lumbering, trapping, and particularly the tourist industry. At that time all roads coming into the North terminated at a dead end.

"As a tourist," I began, "I would not be interested in going back over the same road over country I saw when I came in. Rather, I would want to keep going and return by another road."

Then we got out our maps of northern Saskatchewan—the new detailed aerial photography maps. I took a pencil and in only a few minutes I had marked a line through the part of the country I had travelled while trapping, hunting, fishing, and prospecting and then we discussed a road that

Construction on Hanson Lake Road,
circa 1958.

would link Prince Albert with Flin Flon. Richards took a long quiet look at my pencilled line with a view that it might possibly become that link.

Going back a few years before I drew this likely route, my employer Lew Parres I had asked me to draw a map of the best location for a road to pass near the north end of Hanson Lake. At that time not enough mineralization had been found in the region to warrant a road but Parres had high hopes that one day some of his claims there would become operating mines. I also believed that the area had mining possibilities but when I sketched an access road from Flin Flon to Hanson Lake's shore I did not expect ever to see such a road, but I thought about it from time to time. My road would continue on to link up with the highway to Prince Albert. My dream included the wonderful tourist attraction such a road could become, the sports fishing and big game hunting possibilities it would afford, along with the subdued yet haunting natural beauty of the land that would bring them back time after time. Above all, the benefits to local residents and industry could be invaluable.

One day I read in the *Flin Flon Miner* that I had mapped such a road. In fact, my friend Barry Richards who had submitted the map had included an article to go with it. I was surprised and pleased to read his good report on the location of the road and his reasoning for such a project, which coincided with my own.

I stayed with drilling and prospecting for a time. In this period I talked to several people about the road but they were all of the opinion that I would never see its construction through that area of wilderness as published in the paper. I got to the stage where I very seldom mentioned the road to anybody.

In the summer of 1957 I met Margaret who later became my second wife. I was extremely fortunate to meet her for she is a wonderful companion and makes home what it should be. She never takes the time to complain and has been a real mother to my daughter Marylin. There is a fine family relationship between us; Margaret, Marylin, Margaret's three daughters and myself.

In the winter of 1957–1958 I was on the job freighting supplies to diamond drilling camps at various locations. I used the new vehicle that had proven invaluable for moving freight over frozen swamps, lake ice, and portages; the Bombardier.

To Lew Parres must go the credit of discovering the first commercial mine at Hanson Lake—a rich deposit of zinc, lead, and silver—which was verified at about this time.

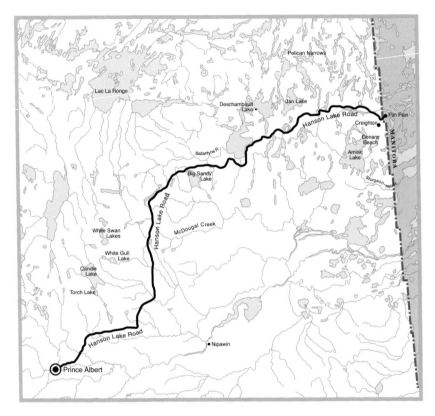

The Hanson Lake Road followed
Olaf Hanson's travels in northern
Saskatchewan over the years.

During the summer of 1958 I was back in the wilderness prospecting and trenching on some of my claims. The latter part of that year I was in the employ of Archie Talbot, a diamond drilling contractor who was then working at Beaver Lake.

When I returned home to Flin Flon I heard the astonishing news that the Construction Branch of the Saskatchewan Department of Natural Resources was building a road from Smeaton, Saskatchewan to Flin Flon, Manitoba! Later I learned that they were starting at Creighton, Saskatchewan. Actually, they were working from both ends.

The fall of 1958 was very wet from seemingly endless rain. One day the road construction foreman and an engineer from Natural Resources paid me a visit. Creighton Creek, they told me, where they planned to cross, was waist deep in water and the banks were too wet and flooding. They asked me to come with them for a day and find a better crossing. I recalled that in the summer of 1931 I had walked around Flin Flon Lake and had crossed Creighton Creek where there was high and dry walking on either side.

With the engineer, I located the crossing. When we returned to Creighton that afternoon, among the construction equipment and trailers I met Hector Breland, project supervisor. He had just returned from Prince Albert and had learned of my locating the dry crossing at Creighton Creek. From that day until the completion of the road, I was employed by Natural Resources as Road Locator and Engineer's Helper.

I was very happy in this position. Besides locating the road from the Manitoba border to South-East Bay of Deschambault Lake, I did the drilling and blasting.

The road is now Saskatchewan Highway 106 and is named "The Hanson Lake Road." The naming of the road is an honour I never expected. I can name, and I know several others, who contributed more than I for the existence of the road. It was, however, a dream come true for me. What had begun with the pencil line on the maps that evening at the drilling camp had become a reality.

The road, when completed, seemed to follow very closely the main trend of my ramblings in northern Saskatchewan over the years. Beginning at the southern end at Smeaton (not very far from Parker's homestead) the Hanson Lake Road touches, crosses, or gives access by branch roads to such familiar geographical features as Bedard Creek, Torch River, White Gull Creek, Fishing Lakes, Caribou Creek, McDougal Creek, Little Bear Lake, Big Sandy Lake, Ballantyne River, Deschambault Lake Settlement and South-East Arm, Tulabi Lake and Tulabi Brook, Limestone Lake, Jan Lake, Mirond Lake, Pelican Narrows, Hanson Lake, the Sturgeon-weir River near Birch Portage, Johnson Lake, Annabel Lake, and finally Amisk (Beaver) Lake.

I, who had covered these places on foot, never imagined I would see so many cars and trucks, holiday vehicles trailing pleasure boats, cars carrying canoes, and all manner of vehicles where I had mushed dogs in winter and packed canoes in summer, fall, and spring. Sometimes we had referred to walking as "using the footmobile" and it was the only way we could traverse the high rocky hills. Our only concern was tires (shoes) for the foot. Our journeys were by canoe on the rivers and from lake to lake, without the benefit of insect repellents...such preparations would be on the market of the future. We kept the mosquitoes away with smudges where we stopped to cook our meals and we always carried mosquito bars to cover our beds at night. Sandflies were particularly troublesome on the portages in the late summer heat.

Not everyone sees a dream come true during his own time. I am one of the fortunate ones who did.

EPILOGUE

I N THE YEARS THAT I prospected, I often located valuable mineral deposits. I never did find a deposit large enough to warrant a mining development. I kept searching for the bonanza that might be just over the next hill. If it was not there, I would then look on the other side of a muskeg where I might find traces of copper or silver or other minerals. This gave me the drive to continue until the summer season ended. All winter I was planning on going further north next summer as surely there was a rich mine there waiting to be found.

When I first got interested in prospecting, back in 1933, I met an old trapper and prospector at Beaver Lake. We were watching two other prospectors who were loading their two canoes with groceries and equipment to go to the Churchill River to look for minerals. Before they left my old companion offered this free advice:

"Boys," he said, "Why don't you stay right in this area and look under your feet instead of walking over mines to look for mines that are far away?"

At that time, we all had a good laugh at his remark but now I know it was most true advice. In that very same area where this advice had been offered, three producing mines were later found. My old friend did not live to see them in a region where he had trapped and prospected for many years.

At the time of writing, we are just beginning to locate the mining wealth of northern Saskatchewan. This is buried by muskeg and lake and overburden. With the advanced techniques of locating minerals, and transportation by air and by road on Highway 106 and Number 2, it is relatively easy to get to mineral country and to prospect.

Anyone who is interested in prospecting has the opportunity to do so, even if he or she is just spending a few days on vacation. Anyone can take a light canoe, tent and camping outfit, and supply of groceries, to gain access to the wilderness where an undiscovered mine surely exists. Plan your load so that there is no unnecessary weight and be prepared to pack from lake to lake. There are prospectors who travel alone but my advice is to travel with one or two others, one of whom should be experienced in such a venture. If there are three in the party, take another small canoe and a small outboard motor to tow it. Plan your journey by taking reliable maps for the area you intend to cover. For anyone who loves the outdoors, it could be a wonderful experience.

From the beginning of my travels in the wilderness until 1934, we had no aerial topographical maps. Our maps of those early times showed only the main rivers and the large lakes. To locate small lakes, I followed small creeks. These creeks would lead me to these small lakes and to larger creeks. I found creeks that ended in vast floating bogs. Sometimes, in spring and summer, I located lakes on a calm evening or early morning by listening to the call of loons. I found several lakes in my time by just following the sound overland. Lakes could also be located by climbing a high hill or a tall tree to sight a lake many miles away. We located lakes for trapping muskrat, beaver, and mink in that manner.

Nowadays, when we go north, we gather our outfit and maps, board a plane which puts us down on some small remote lake where there is a good camping place along with a small canoe so we can get around. We leave word with the pilot when he is to return to take us back or on to another location. Then we set up our tent and in a short time, we may be eating fresh-caught fish with our first meal. After a good dinner, we can unfold our maps and locate lakes by the dozen in only a few minutes.

The arrival of modern day maps ended the climbing of trees and hills and listening to the loons as methods of finding lakes.

During the early 1930s while I lived in the Pelican Narrows country, I was among the natives. All our neighbours were native trappers. I enjoyed their company and they were wonderful friends. Any time there was any interesting news, it was brought by those who came to visit. We

One of Olaf Hanson's proudest
moments, at his very own roadside
historical marker near Gillingham Lake,
September 17, 1975.

called it "the moccasin telegraph" in those days. I was always welcome at their homes and they were likewise welcome at our camp. I never locked my cabin door and I never had anything stolen. Any time we met while travelling, we stopped to make a cup of tea. If I had lunch, I divided it with them, as they did if I had none. We had a lot of fun around a cozy camp fire while sitting on our loaded toboggans with our moccasined feet on a bed of spruce boughs to keep our footwear dry. They always had a nickname for certain individuals, a nickname that stays with the person all his life. Here are a few examples—one chap they called "Pe Peto" which meant "Much Smoke" for that man seemed to always be smoking; another was "Min Sap We" meaning "Jam," an item the chap loved to eat; another was "Ki Kiki Magees" meaning "Has nothing—is very poor." I once had a fisherman working for me who let his beard grow. His name was Gerald but the natives dubbed him "Mistawan" meaning "Whiskers."

About forty per cent of these people spoke English. Therefore, I had to learn the Cree language. I managed to learn enough to understand what they were asking me and I did manage to keep a conversation going. They became immensely entertained when I got so I could tell them stories in Cree but I never mastered the language altogether.

I have a lot of good memories of the natives and I miss their friendship and sense of humour.

As far back as I can remember, I always liked people. No one, regardless of his race, colour, nationality, or creed was a stranger for very long. It was a great pleasure to meet people and to learn of their problems and become their friend. Today, it is a great pleasure indeed to meet any of these people once again as old friends.

End of the Trail

INDEX